CliffsNotes™
Buying and
Selling on eBay®

By Greg Holden

IN THIS BOOK

- Find what you're looking for, from antique toys to classic cars
- Watch the auctions strategically and place bids at the right time
- Make the items you sell attractive to prospective bidders
- Protect yourself from fraud
- Reinforce what you learn with CliffsNotes Review
- Find more Internet information in CliffsNotes Resource Center and online at www.cliffsnotes.com

IDG Books Worldwide, Inc.

An International Data Group Company

Foster City, CA • Chicago, IL • Indianapolis, IN • New York, NY

ID(
BOO
WORLDW

D0818684

About the Author

Greg Holden is the founder and president of Stylus Media, a print and electronic media design firm. He has authored eleven books, including *Internet Auctions For Dummies* (IDG Books Worldwide, Inc.).

Publisher's Acknowledgments

Editorial

Senior Project Editor: Kyle Looper
Acquisitions Editor: Joyce Pepple
Senior Copy Editor: William Barton
Technical Editor: Matthew McClure

Production

Indexer: York Production Services, Inc.
Proofreader: York Production Services, Inc.
IDG Books Indianapolis Production Department

CliffsNotes™ Buying and Selling on eBay
Published by
IDG Books Worldwide, Inc.
An International Data Group Company
919 E. Hillsdale Blvd.
Suite 400
Foster City, CA 94404
www.idgbooks.com (IDG Books Worldwide Web site)
www.cliffsnotes.com (CliffsNotes Web site)

Library of Congress Catalog Card No.: 99-64596
ISBN: 0-7645-8528-2
Printed in the United States of America
10 9 8 7 6 5 4 3 2 1
1O/RW/RR/ZZ/IN
Distributed in the United States by IDG Books Worldwide, Inc.
Distributed by CDG Books Canada Inc. for Canada; by Transworld Publishers Limited in the United Kingdom; by IDG Norge Books for Norway; by IDG Sweden Books for Sweden; by IDG Books Australia Publishing Corporation Pty. Ltd. for Australia and New Zealand; by TransQuest Publishers Pte Ltd. for Singapore, Malaysia, Thailand, Indonesia, and Hong Kong; by Gotop Information Inc. for Taiwan; by ICG Muse, Inc. for Japan; by Intersoft for South Africa; by Eyrolles for France; by International Thomson Publishing for Germany, Austria and Switzerland; by Distribuidora Cuspide for Argentina; by LR International for Brazil; by Galileo Libros for Chile; by Ediciones ZETA S.C.R. Ltda. for Peru; by WS Computer Publishing Corporation, Inc., for the Philippines; by Contemporanea de Ediciones for Venezuela; by Express Computer Distributors for the Caribbean and West Indies; by Micronesia Media Distributor, Inc. for Micronesia; by Chips Computadoras S.A. de C.V. for Mexico; by Editorial Norma de Panama S.A. for Panama; by American Bookshops for Finland.

For general information on IDG Books Worldwide's books in the U.S., please call our Consumer Customer Service department at **800-762-2974**. For reseller information, including discounts and premium sales, please call our Reseller Customer Service department at **800-434-3422**.

For information on where to purchase IDG Books Worldwide's books outside the U.S., please contact our International Sales department at 317-596-5530 or fax **317-596-5692**.

For consumer information on foreign language translations, please contact our Customer Service department at **1-800-434-3422**, fax **317-596-5692**, or e-mail rights@idgbooks.com.

For information on licensing foreign or domestic rights, please phone +1-650-655-3109.

For sales inquiries and special prices for bulk quantities, please contact our Sales department at 650-655-3200 or write to the address above.

For information on using IDG Books Worldwide's books in the classroom or for ordering examination copies, please contact our Educational Sales department at **800-434-2086** or fax **317-596-5499**.

For press review copies, author interviews, or other publicity information, please contact our Public Relations department at **650-655-3000** or fax **650-655-3299**.

For authorization to photocopy items for corporate, personal, or educational use, please contact Copyright Clearance Center, 222 Rosewood Drive, Danvers, MA 01923, or fax **978-750-4470**.

Table of Contents

INTRODUCTION

Have you ever experienced the thrill of finding an incredible bargain at a specialty store or been amazed at what people are willing to pay for things that you might toss in the garbage? If so, then you'll want to learn about eBay — the hottest auction site on the Internet. And CliffsNotes *Buying and Selling on eBay* is the shortest distance to eBay proficiency.

Why Do You Need This Book?

Can you answer yes to any of these questions?

- Do you need to learn about eBay fast?
- Don't have time to read 500 pages on Internet auctions?
- Do you want to find a gift at a bargain price?
- Do you want to expand an existing business to a whole new range of customers via the Internet?

If so, then CliffsNotes *Buying and Selling on eBay* is for you!

How to Use This Book

You can read this book straight through or just look for the information you need. You can find information on a particular topic in a number of ways: You can search the index in the back of the book, locate your topic in the Table of Contents, or read the In This Chapter list in each chapter. To reinforce your learning, check out the Review and the Resource Center at the back of the book. To help you find important information in the book, look for the following icons in the text:

This icon alerts you to something dangerous or to avoid.

This icon clues you in to helpful hints and advice.

This icon points out something worth keeping in mind.

Don't Miss Our Web Site

Keep up with the changing world of the Internet by visiting our Web site at www.cliffsnotes.com. Here's what you'll find:

- Interactive tools that are fun and informative
- Links to interesting Web sites
- Additional resources to help you continue your learning

At www.cliffsnotes.com you can even register for a new feature called CliffsNotes Daily, which offers you newsletters on a variety of topics, delivered right to your e-mail inbox each business day.

If you haven't discovered the Internet and are wondering how to get online, pick up *Getting on the Internet*, new from Cliffs-Notes. You'll learn just what you need to make your online connection quickly and easily. See you at www.cliffs-notes.com!

CHAPTER 1
EXPLORING THE WORLD OF EBAY

IN THIS CHAPTER

- Comparing online and regular auctions
- Getting your gear together
- Checking out the eBay home page
- Mastering the eBay interface

eBay has brought down the gavel and come away as the big winner in the competitive field of Internet auctions. Whether you're looking for new ways to find bargains or hoping to make some extra money by selling your stuff, the best place to start is at eBay, the most popular and successful of all online auction services.

Because so many shoppers flock to eBay, the site offers more resources for both buyers and sellers than any other service can. The abundance of eBay auction sales gives shoppers a great chance of finding a bargain, an unusual object, or a rare collectible. And because so many people shop on eBay, sellers have a great chance of getting top dollar for their merchandise.

Comparing eBay to Traditional Auctions

Most people are familiar with traditional auctions either through first-hand experience or by seeing them in movies or on TV. A great way to begin to understand how eBay works is to compare its operation to that of a traditional auction house, such as Sotheby's or Christie's. I compare these two types of auctions in Table 1-1.

Table 1-1: **Differences between eBay and Traditional Auctions**

At a Traditional Auction House	At eBay
The auction takes place at a given time, and everyone bids together.	Participants submit bids online over a certain period of time (usually 3–7 days); the location of buyer and seller doesn't matter with regard to the bidding.
The auctioneer photographs each item, and a description and photo appears in a sales catalog.	The seller photographs the items and posts the presentations and descriptions online.
Bidders can (usually) touch, examine, and otherwise interact with the items on display.	Bidders can't touch what they want to buy. They can, however, see the item online and e-mail questions to the seller.
Expert appraisers are available to examine the sales items and advise both buyers and sellers of their worth.	Buyers and sellers can access a huge database of information and must make their own appraisals about the value of items.
Auctioneers offer one-of-a-kind or very rare items to an exclusive clientele.	eBay offers Items and collectibles to a huge group of collectors, bargain hunters, and prospective buyers.

Participants on eBay must function as their own appraisers and auctioneers. If you plan to sell, learn how to create high-quality images and enticing descriptions that you provide for each item up for auction as described in Chapters 8 and 9. They will be crucial elements in interesting prospective buyers.

Getting Ready to Connect

Getting started with eBay is easy — and, even better, the service is free. If you plan to access eBay solely as a buyer, you don't need any particular software or hardware beyond the basic setup that you use for standard Web-surfing, as the following list describes:

- A computer with a monitor and either a dialup (modem) or a high-speed (such as cable modem) connection to the Internet.

- An account with a company that connects you to the Internet — typically, an *Internet service provider* (ISP) such as MindSpring Enterprises or a commercial online service such as America Online. If you've never connected to the Internet, check out *Getting on the Internet,* new from CliffsNotes, to find the shortest distance to the Internet.

- An e-mail address (eBay, as well as individual buyers and sellers, need this address to communicate with you) and e-mail software.

- A Web browser, which is simply a program that you use for viewing Web-page content. Most operating systems come with a Web browser (probably Netscape Navigator or Microsoft Internet Explorer) preinstalled. Your browser enables you to shop for items that eBay offers for sale or publish your own sales information on eBay's Web site.

To sell items through online auctions, you also need some additional hardware and software for capturing or editing digital images of your merchandise (see Chapter 9).

Docking Your Browser at eBay

After you secure the necessary equipment and establish your Internet connection, it's time to embark on your online auction adventure. Get started by loading up your trusty Web browser and tracking down eBay's Web site (www.ebay.com). Follow these steps:

1. Establish your Internet connection. Because the directions for doing so vary depending on your ISP, check with your ISP for details.

    If you connect to the Internet by using an external modem, make sure it is turned on before you try to establish your Internet connection.

2. Start your Web Browser software. Most Web browsers place an icon on your desktop, so double-click this icon. The browser window opens and connects you to your home page.

3. Click in the Address box (Internet Explorer) or the Location box (Navigator) to select the *URL* (uniform resource locator or Web address) that's already in it. Press the Delete key to get rid of that URL.

4. Type the URL for eBay's home page (www.ebay.com) in the Address box and press the Enter key. Your browser connects to eBay's Web site, and the eBay home page appears, as shown in Figure 1-1.

You can go straight to eBay every time you start your Web browser by designating the site as your home page. Find your Web browser and perform the steps below:

■ **Netscape Navigator:** Choose Edit⇨Preferences, click Navigator, and enter www.ebay.com in the Location box.

■ **Internet Explorer for Windows:** Choose Tools⇨Internet Options, click the General tab, and enter www.ebay.com in the Address box.

■ **Internet Explorer for Mac:** Choose Edit⇨Preferences and click the Home/Search button under Web Browser. Enter www.ebay.com in the Address box.

Figure 1-1:   eBay's home page is a good starting point for both buyers and sellers.

Click here for a
list of the site's
main pages

Search for an item by
entering keywords here

| home | my eBay | site map |

| Browse | Sell | Services | Search | Help | Community |

eBay™

your personal trading community™

[search] tips

welcome

categories

Antiques (60266)
Books, Movies, Music (345370)
Coins & Stamps (92814)
Collectibles (776250)
Computers (87138)
Dolls, Figures (48947)
Jewelry, Gemstones (95367)
Photo & Electronics (44436)
Pottery & Glass (151552)
Sports Memorabilia

Sell your
item

new users
Click here

Get news
and chat

Register
It's free and fun

featurEd

*Epson Sc 440/640/740 Color Inkjet Cartridge
Mercedes 300sel Legal Notice / No Reserve
1000+ Windows Games For Your Computer Cd !!
2 Ricky Martin Tix~San Jose,Ca~1st Level!

What is eBay?
How do I bid?
How do I sell?
Register, it's free!

statS

2,473,978 items for sale
in 1,627 categories
now!

Over 1.5 billion page
views per month!

fun sTuff

Subscribe
now!

Click here
for user
tutorials

Click here
to set up an
account

Getting around the eBay Interface

You can't go prospecting for treasure unless you have a map
and you know how to read it. eBay's Web site is the map, and
the three big features that function like fingers pointing you
along the way on your treasure hunt are the central clickable
images, the navigation bar, and the Site Map page.

The central images

A great way to get started on eBay is by clicking the images
labeled `Sell your item`, `Get news and chat`, `new
users Click here`, and `Register it's free and`

fun in the center of the home page. Each image is a click-able link that takes you to an area of the eBay site that's especially useful for new users:

■ **Sell your item:** Clicking this image connects you to the eBay Sell Your Item page, which presents you with a form you can fill out and submit to eBay that starts an eBay auction, as explained in Chapter 8. (You need an eBay ID and password before you can buy or sell an item.)

■ **Get news and chat:** Clicking this image takes you to a page that explains how to communicate with other eBay users (see Chapter 7).

■ **New users click here:** Clicking on this image takes you to the Help Basics page, which contains links to help for new users. Scroll to the bottom of the page to find tutorials on common eBay topics.

■ **Register it's free and fun:** Clicking on this image whisks you off to an area where you can obtain an eBay ID and password that allow you to participate in eBay auctions. See Chapter 2 for the signing-up details.

The navigation bar

The navigation bar at the top of the home page offers categories that make it easy to do the things you probably want to do on eBay: Browse, Sell, Services, Help, Search, and Community.

The same navigation bar appears on virtually all eBay pages to help you know where you are and to help you find your way around.

Clicking in any of the boxes on the navigation bar takes you to a different part of eBay's site. Each navigation box has its own subcategories, which appear as boxes beneath a main navigation category that you click.

For example, if you click Help, you go to the main Help page. The main Help page has its own subnavigation bar, which contains a new second set of categories. Each of these is a link to a more specific help-related page.

Table 1-2 explains how the links in the main section of the navigation bar function.

Table 1-2:   eBay's Navigation Bar

Link	Where It Takes You	What It Does	See Chapter
Browse	eBay Main Categories page	Contains links to featured eBay auctions as well as a list of eBay's main auction categories.	2 and 3
Sell	Sell Your Item page	Contains a form you can fill out and submit to eBay to start your own auction.	8, 9, and 10
Services	Services Overview	Describes eBay services that help you find what you want, resolve disputes, and feedback comments that have been left for eBay buyers and sellers.	5
Search	eBay Search for Items page	Contains a variety of formsyou can fill out to find exactly the auction item you're looking for.	3
Help	Help Overview page	Includes a search box where you can locate a topic you want to explore, as well as links to specific Help topics.	

(continued)

Table 1-2: eBay's Navigation Bar *(continued)*

Link	Where It Takes You	What It Does	See Chapter
Community	Community Overview page	Contains links to message boards, the eBay life newsletter, and other resources for interacting with other eBay users.	7

The Site Map page

eBay's Web site is pretty extensive, so finding documents that cover such specific topics as insurance, appraisals, and how to post multiple items for sale simultaneously can sometimes prove difficult.

If you need help finding anything specific, just click the site map link, which appears in the list of links at the top of virtually every eBay page. Your browser then connects to the Site Map page shown in Figure 1-2. The Site Map page includes links to all areas of the eBay site.

Figure 1-2: The eBay site map provides links to every main eBay page.

CHAPTER 2

REGISTERING AND STARTING TO BID

IN THIS CHAPTER

- Becoming an eBay registered user
- Picking the type of eBay auction that's right for you
- Exchanging e-mail with sellers and placing your first bids

You can get a good idea of how the eBay system works by sitting on the sidelines and watching the traders buy and sell. Before long, however, you'll be ready to make the move from spectator to active eBay participant. This chapter describes how to register with eBay so you can start buying and selling.

The goal of this chapter is to show you how to place your first bids on eBay auctions. You first need to register with eBay and then choose among the different types of sales that eBay offers before you can start your actual bidding. The following sections tell you how to get going.

Registering with eBay

Eager as you may be to get going, you can't simply start trading on eBay; you must first provide eBay and its users with enough information to contact you if necessary. You don't need to submit a great deal of personal information, but you must give eBay your real name and address. Follow these easy steps to set up a registered eBay account (eBay):

1. Go to the eBay home page. (See Chapter 1 for details.)

2. Click the Register It's Free and Fun image in the center of the eBay home page, or on the <u>Register, it's free!</u> hyperlink under the Welcome heading. (You must be 18 to register.) The eBay – To Register, First Choose Your Country Web page appears.

   If you use Version 3.0 or later of Netscape Navigator or Internet Explorer, then select the check box labeled `Click on the box to the left to register using SSL`. *SSL* (Secure Sockets Layer) encrypts any sensitive data that you send to eBay to prevent snoops from getting your personal information. It costs nothing in time or money to use SSL; the browser and Web server handle the encryption and decoding behind the scenes.

3. Click your country's name in the drop-down list of countries that appears in the middle of the eBay - To Register, First Choose Your Country page. Then click the Begin the Registration Process Now button. The eBay Registration page appears.

4. Enter your name, address, phone numbers, and e-mail address in the appropriate text boxes on the initial registration form. You don't need to fill out any of the information in the Optional Info area of the form. (*AOL users:* Pay close attention to the instructions on this page that are especially for you so that your data reaches eBay successfully.)

5. Click the Continue button at the bottom of the page. A Web page appears displaying the data you just filled out so that you can review it before submitting it to eBay (see Figure 2-1).

Figure 2-1: Review your personal information and read all instructions carefully before submitting your registration to eBay.

Please Review The Following Information

E-mail address	gregholden57@x85.com	to be verified in Step 2
Full name	John Q. Public	OK
Address	1234 Wistful Vista	OK
City	Los Angeles	OK
State	CA	OK
Zip Code	60002	OK
Country	United States	OK
Primary phone #	(312) 455 - 2343	OK

6. Click the submit hyperlink. A Registration - Step 1 Complete Web page appears. It includes instructions reminding you that you can't start buying or selling until you receive an e-mail message from eBay with a special number that lets you confirm your registration. You can explore eBay until you receive the confirmation.

7. Ensure that you're connected to the Internet and enter the Web address for the eBay confirmation page into your browser (`http://pages.ebay.com/US/services/registration/reg-confirm.html`). You can also click the Confirmation Registration Form link on the Registration – Step 1 Complete page.

8. Read the User Agreement on the confirmation page that appears and then click the I Accept button at the bottom of the page. A Step 3 - Confirm Your Registration: Part 2 of 2 Web page appears.

Watch your e-mail Inbox for a confirmation message from eBay. (You should receive this message within 24 hours.) This message contains a confirmation number that you should write down. When you receive the message, proceed as follows:

1. Enter your name, confirmation number, and a new password in the appropriate boxes on this page.

2. Click the Complete Your Registration button. A Web page appears confirming that you're successfully registered with eBay. You can now start to surf and place bids with the service.

A good password contains seven or more characters and a mixture of letters and numerals. For added security, you can also mix uppercase and lowercase letters, such as *ebT2fd7.* Don't make your password too complicated and do write it in a secure place (somewhere where people can't find it easily, such as the back of a file folder) immediately. If you lose your password, you can go to the eBay Help pages (click **Help** on the navigation bar) and select a new one.

Enter a *username* in the User ID text box near the bottom of this page if you want to use a short, user-friendly nickname that others see online. If you don't enter a name here, your e-mail address serves as your username. (A username looks somewhat more personal than an e-mail address.)

Picking the Auction That's Right for You

Auctions on eBay come in many different varieties, but the "standard" auctions (that is, those that aren't in a featured or other special category) are the ones that most everyday collectors and shoppers frequent. You can find a list of all of them — including more than 350 at any given time — by clicking <u>home</u> ☞ <u>site map</u> ☞ <u>Category Overview</u>.

Some auctions last a week; some last ten days; some last only three days. The seller of an item determines how long the auction can last. If the seller decides the auction will last one week, the sale ends exactly seven days (to the exact minute and second) from the time the sale was posted on eBay. Until that time, anyone can bid and rebid on the item. The seller does have the right to end the sale early, but this doesn't happen often because it can hurt the seller's reputation.

Some sellers pay an extra fee to feature their sales in a special category (see Figure 2-2).

Figure 2-2:   Featured auctions are collected in a special category, and some appear on eBay's home page.

Featured Auctions		You are on page **1** of 18.	Next Page ▸	
Current		🗎 = Gallery 📷 = Picture ⚡ = Hot! ✦ = New!		
Status	**Item**	**Price**	**Bids**	**Ends PDT**
📷 ✦	BEST GOLF GAME! MICROSOFT GOLF 99! 2-CDS SET! ⚡	$15.00	-	08/10 16:56
✦	Never Get a Speeding Ticket Again ~Photo-No~ ⚡	$11.95	-	08/13 16:53
🗎 📷 ✦	200MMX upgrade for older Pentiums! V/MC/AE	$59.00	-	08/13 16:48
📷 ✦	ASTONISHING TALES #2 - 10 PG. KIRBY STORY!	$1499.99	-	08/10 16:48
✦	RAREST POKEMON Cards EVER~Sealed Boxes~Dutch	$44.99	-	08/13 16:46

Standard and Nonstandard Auctions

The basic eBay auction formats fall into a few simple classifications. Table 2-1 provides brief explanations of each category of auction that you find on eBay.

Table 2-1: Types of auctions on eBay

Type of auction	Explanation
Standard auction	A typical auction lasts for 3–10 days. The seller specifies a minimum bid, and bidding goes up by increments. A reserve price may or may not be specified (see below). The sale item goes to the high bidder at the time the auction ends.
Reserve price auction	A measure of protection that a seller can add to any type of auction (standard, private, featured). The reserve price is the lowest price at which a seller is willing to sell an item. Usually kept secret from bidders. If no one meets the reserve price, the seller needn't sell the item.
Dutch auction	This format is used to auction multiple, identical items. The seller specifies the minimum price (the starting bid) and the number of items available. Potential buyers can bid at or above that minimum for the quantity in which they're interested. At the close of the auction, all winning bidders pay the same price as the lowest qualifying bidder. (Qualifying bidders are those who have bid above the minimum price and whose place in the bidding hierarchy matches the number of items available.)
Private auction	A type of sale that a seller can specify to auction "adult" items in which bidders don't disclose their e-mail addresses on the item screen or bidding history screen. You need a credit card on file with eBay to both view and bid on items in these auctions. Additionally, sellers can't list adult items for private auctions without credit card verification.

Dutch auctions can be confusing. Read more about them on eBay's site at `pages.ebay.com/aw/help/help-g-dutch-auction.html`. An experienced eBay user offers some good Dutch auction tips at `www.frii.com/~afs/ebay`.

Featured Auctions

Along with the general types of auction arrangements that I describe in the preceding list, eBay also provides you with various ways to call attention to (or "feature") your own particular item for sale. Featuring an item in some of these specialized categories costs extra for sellers, and the merchandise in such sales tend to cost the buyer more, too. But you can often find items in these featured categories that you just can't locate anywhere else.

I list the various ways that you can feature an item in an eBay auction in Table 2-2. Most featured auctions require the seller to pay an extra fee above and beyond the $2.50 listing fee that all sales require (as this book goes to press). The table includes the fee as well.

Table 2-2:   Featured Auctions on eBay

Type of Auction	Description	Fee (if required)
Featured Auction	Featured Auction listings appear at the top of the main Listings page, which you can access from the menu bar at the top of every page on eBay. eBay randomly selects Featured Auctions to appear in the Featured display area on the main eBay Home page.	$99.95
Category Featured Auctions	Category Featured Auctions appear at the top of the first Web page for the eBay category in which they fall.	$14.95
Big Ticket Items	These items are especially high-priced objects — such as rare automobiles or jerseys signed by sports stars — that go for several thousand dollars and up.	n/a

(continued)

Table 2-2: Featured Auctions on eBay *(continued)*

Type of Auction	Description	Fee (if required)
Gift Section	A gift icon appears along with the listing title for such items, and all items in this category appear in a separate list on a special page (pages.ebay.com/aw/ gift-section.html).	$1
The Gallery	For an extra fee, you can list your auction in eBay's gallery, which lets shoppers brows through items for sale by viewing small "thumbnail" images of what's for sale. You need to submit an image of your item for sale. Items within the Gallery can be featured, too. Find out more at pages. ebay.com/help/sellerguide/ gallery-faq.html.	.25
Club99 Auctions	These auctions, originally started by a group of eBay users, take place the second Saturday of every month. Sellers offer merchandise at an opening price of 99 cents with no reserve price. The auctions last a week. Find out more at members. ebay.com/aboutme/ club99.	n/a
Premium Auctions	At this writing, eBay just announced that it purchased the prestigious auction house Butterfield and Butterfield and that, as a result, users can now access higher end items as well as access Butterfield's appraisal services.	TBA

Shopping and Placing Your First Bids

To get started with eBay, feel free to explore the site the way a savvy shopper explores a big department store or mall: first take a look around and see what's available. Then concentrate on the sales that interest you most and fit your budget.

A great way to get going is to search for items that you collect yourself and know well or that you're particularly interested in. See how many items are being offered for sale and observe how the bidding proceeds. Don't bid on anything for the first day or two. Ask a seller a question about an item you want. After you get a feel for what's being offered and have contacted a seller, you can start to place your own bids.

eBay provides a series of helpful tutorials on registering, bidding, finding items, and other topics. Each one takes only a few minutes and helps you find answers to basic questions. Click <u>home</u> ☞ <u>Help</u> ☞ <u>Tutorials</u> to access the Tutorials page and choose the topic you're interested in.

Bidding on an eBay auction item is easy — so easy that I strongly advise you to research any merchandise in which you're interested before bidding on it, as I describe in Chapter 5. Auctions typically last for several days, so take enough time to be sure your bid is reasonable for the item you want and represents an amount you can afford.

Each sales listing on eBay appears on its own Web page. Typically, the price and seller information appears at the top of the page. Beneath this information, the page includes the User ID and bid of the current high bidder. Below bid information, you find a photo and description of the item. Under the description, you find the minimum bid you want to place to be the next high bidder.

To place a bid on eBay, follow these steps:

1. Locate the item you want to bid on either by entering its name in the Search box that appears on virtually all eBay pages and clicking the Search button, or by clicking through categories until you find the item you want. (See Chapter 3 for more.) Scroll down to the Enter your maximum bid box at the bottom of the page on which the auction item itself appears (see Figure 2-3).

Figure 2-3: Each item for auction on eBay appears on its own Web page, which includes a bid submission form.

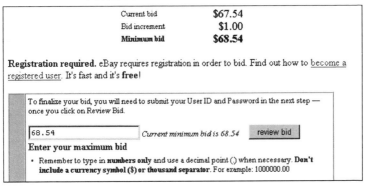

Current bid	$67.54
Bid increment	$1.00
Minimum bid	**$68.54**

Registration required. eBay requires registration in order to bid. Find out how to <u>become a registered user</u>. It's fast and it's **free**!

To finalize your bid, you will need to submit your User ID and Password in the next step — once you click on Review Bid.

| 68.54 | *Current minimum bid is 68.54* | review bid |

Enter your maximum bid

- Remember to type in **numbers only** and use a decimal point (.) when necessary. **Don't include a currency symbol ($) or thousand separator**. For example: 1000000.00

2. Enter the amount you want to bid in the box above the words `Enter your maximum bid`. You don't need to enter the dollar sign ($), but enter the decimal point to ensure that eBay receives the correct bid amount. If you want to bid $10, for example, enter **10.00**.

3. Click the Review Bid button. A Web page (entitled `Review bid for...`) appears that enables you to review your bid before you actually submit it to eBay.

4. Enter your eBay User ID and password in the User ID and Password boxes near the top of the Review Bid For page. This page also contains a link to the seller's feedback profile (click on the seller's User ID under the list entitled `A few useful tips...`). To submit your bid to eBay, click the Place Bid button beneath the User ID and Password boxes.

5. A page entitled `eBay Confirming Bid for Item` appears. This page confirms that your bid has been received and tells you whether or not you are the high bidder. Scroll down this page to see the top half of the auction listing with the high bid displayed. If you are the high bidder, your name and new high bid appears on the Web page. (If your name doesn't appear as the high bidder, you're probably up against a proxy bidder — see Chapter 4 for details.)

If someone outbids you while the sale is still going on, you'll receive an e-mail message so that you can place another bid if you want to. If you win, you'll receive an e-mail message from eBay after the auction ends informing you of the good news.

CHAPTER 3
SEARCHING FOR THE GOODS YOU WANT

IN THIS CHAPTER

- Drilling through categories of auction merchandise
- Searching for items by using eBay's Classifieds Search page
- Researching past sales by searching completed auctions
- Using eBay search shortcuts and tips

Have you ever found yourself at a flea market or garage sale, eagerly scanning long tables full of rare hatpins, campaign buttons, duck lures, and other strange items, wishing you could simply put your finger on exactly the treasure you want? Believe it or not, you can do it at eBay. If you're looking for a rare porcelain mynah bird bookend, you and the seller of that bookend can find one another amid all the auction listings for vintage pottery, costume jewelry, and electronics equipment that flood the eBay site each day.

Searching for sales information on eBay is an essential part of both buying and selling. Your eBay experience depends, to some extent, on whether you can find what you want quickly or whether you need to look long and hard through pages and lists before you find that special something. The goal of this chapter is to familiarize you with the two ways to locate sales data on eBay and to help you find what you're looking for with a minimum of time and effort.

Looking through eBay Auction Categories

eBay provides you with tools that let you search through thousands of objects at auction from the comfort of your computer. eBay's computers index the current list of sales constantly, but you still may not find the most recent items because many fall into more than one possible category. eBay provides you with an alternative by letting you browse through several hundred possible categories in which to find or list merchandise. You can view all of these categories on the eBay Category Overview page (click <u>site map</u> ☞ <u>Category Overview</u>).

Remember

Keep in mind that sellers choose the categories in which their sale items appear. Many sellers pick a category containing objects that are similar to those they're selling. Shoppers, therefore, are more likely to bid on the item, because they're already interested in the types of item in that category. Still, the process of categorizing items for auction isn't an exact science.

Explore eBay's auction categories when you don't know exactly what you're looking for but you have a general idea of where to start. Suppose you're looking for a gift for someone who's interested in photography, but you've forgotten the exact type of equipment the person uses. Start with the most general type of information (the link Photo & Electronics on eBay's home page). When the Photo & Electronics page appears, click your way through the subcategories — which become progressively more specific — until you find the one containing what you seek.

You're probably already used to exploring the levels of information within your public library. If you're looking for a detective novel, you may start with the fiction area, which provides the broadest possible selection of novels, and work your way down to a specific book by Dashiell Hammett, for instance.

On eBay, you can access auction categories from one of the following two starting points:

■ **The eBay home page (at** www.ebay.com**).** The home page lists a few of the more popular categories. If you're looking for a video camera, for example, you can locate one by accessing eBay's home page and then clicking <u>Photo & Electronics</u> ☞ <u>Photo Equipment</u>. After the Photo Equipment page appears (as shown in Figure 3-1), you can then click links that enable you to browse through more than 300 Web pages full of listings, looking for the camera you want.

■ **The eBay site map (click the site map link at the top of any eBay Web page).** The site map functions as a sort of card catalog for the entire eBay site and includes the <u>CategoryOverview</u> link. Click this link and you access a Web page that contains the complete list of eBay categories. The list is quite extensive and, if you have a slower dialup connection, can take many seconds to appear in its entirety.

Viewing the complete list at least once is useful, however, if only for a complete look at the wide range of merchandise available on the site — including items in some unusual categories that you otherwise may overlook, such as Weird Stuff or Hawaiiana.

The advantage of clicking your way through categories is that you may just find information you'd never encounter on your own, especially if you focus only on a single category all the time. And if you're a seller, the category pages can give you an idea of the types of items that you can find in various categories that are similar to yours; you may, in fact, discover some unexpected surprises there.

Figure 3-1: Shutter bugs may enjoy browsing around the Photo Equipment category.

Warning

As eBay categories become crowded with hundreds of listings, the approach of clicking through categories becomes less efficient and, occasionally, simply unworkable. If the merchandise you hope to locate falls within a popular category (for example, Antiques or any of its subcategories, such as Antiques:General or Antiques:Metalware:Silver), you can even find yourself facing a category containing 30, 40, or many more Web pages of auction titles to scan.

Keep in mind that the typical list of auctions on eBay contains as many as 90 separate items and you can easily end up with 800 to 1,000 auctions to look through. Using one of eBay's search options to narrow down your quest can prove far more efficient than exploring categories. I describe these options in the next section.

Searching by Using eBay's Search Feature

When you know exactly what you're looking for, it doesn't make sense to sift through categories guessing where the seller listed it. In these cases, use eBay's Search feature. You find a

Search box right at the top of the eBay site's home page, as well as on the various category pages that I mention in the preceding section.

If you want to look through auctions that have already been completed or search all of a seller's current auctions, you can also access a specific search form (a Web page where you enter and submit a word or phrase you want to find). The following sections describe the various ways you can search for items on eBay, along with tips on searching more efficiently.

Search the eBay home page

eBay enables you to search through its list of current auction titles right from its home page (at www.ebay.com). If, for example, you're in a hurry to get a price on a Sony Mavica camera that's currently for sale, you can follow these steps:

1. Go to the eBay home page and enter the words **Sony Mavica** in the Search text box at the top of the page.

2. Click the Search button. In a few seconds, one of eBay's Web servers returns to your Web browser a new Web page containing a list of all pages that include the words **Sony Mavica** in their title (see Figure 3-2).

Searching with the Find Items page

A more powerful way to locate information is to use the eBay search form, which goes by the name eBay Find Items page (at http://pages.ebay.com/search/items/search.html). You can access this search form by clicking the **Search** link on the navigation bar. The eBay Find Items page enables you to search for current auctions and also has a Completed Search feature that enables you to locate sale prices from completed auctions (see Chapter 4).

Figure 3-2: You may find not one but as many as 50 items on a page of search results that match your criteria.

138235915	SONY MAVICA MVC-FD73 new in box sealed	**$420.00**	5	in 3 mins
139286861	SONY Carrying Case for Mavica FD 91** RARE **	**$46.25**	7	08/03 21:30
136672372	SONY Mavica MVC-FD81 Digital Camera w/Warrant **Pic**	**$550.00**	22	08/03 21:35
139293729	SONY MAVICA MVC-FD-81 DIGITAL CAMERA/"NEW"	**$580.00**	11	08/03 21:46
140205223	L@@K! Sony Mavica NP-F550 InfoLITHIUM Battery **Pic**	**$46.99**	3	08/03 22:55
139316651	Sony Mavica Digital Camera carrying case FD **Pic**	**$14.00**	3	08/03 23:03
140207047	Genuine SONY Soft Carrying Case for Mavica	**$16.00**	7	08/03 23:04
140204442	Sony Mavica FD83 Digital Camera New in Box,	**$600.00**	1	08/04

If you want to limit your search to a certain area (for instance, if you want to arrange with the seller to pick up an item in person and don't want to travel far) use eBay's new regional search feature. Click on the **Search** link in the navigation bar to connect to the eBay Classifieds Search page. Then click on the regional search link in the phrase New regional search feature near the top of the page.

If you plan to search on eBay regularly, make sure that you read the site's search tips (at pages.ebay.com/aw/tips-search.html). This list is pretty extensive; Table 3-1 provides a selection of some of the more useful strategies for narrowing a search.

Table 3-1: eBay Search Tips

Type of Match	What It Does	Example	What It Returns
Exact	Matches an exact series of words or a phrase that you have enclosed in quotation marks	"Montblanc Meisterstuck 149"	Only auction listings that contain the exact phrase Montblanc Meisterstuck 149
OR	Matches any auction listings that include any of a series of words separated by commas with no blank spaces	Montblanc,Meisterstuck	Auction listings that contain the words Montblanc or Meisterstuck
AND	Matches any auction listings that include all of a series of words separated only by a blank space	Montblanc Meisterstuck	Only auction listings that contain both the words Montblanc and Meisterstuck, not necessarily in that order
Exclude words	Excludes any words that occur after a blank space and minus sign	Montblanc –Meisterstuck	Only auction listings that contain the word Montblanc but not the word Meisterstuck

Be careful if you decide to enclose search terms in quotation marks: You run the risk of excluding auctions for the type of item you want but with a description that doesn't match the search terms exactly. In the preceding examples, a search for **"Montblanc Meisterstuck 149"** would fail to return an auction listing for a pen that the listing describes as a "Model 149 Montblanc Meisterstuck."

CHAPTER 4

BEING A SMART SHOPPER

IN THIS CHAPTER

- Researching items before you bid
- Searching for the merchandise you want
- Using proxy bidding to protect your bid
- Sniping and other bid strategies

Most people get started with online auctions as shoppers. They're hoping to pay less for something they need or discover a rare object to add to a collection.

As more shoppers compete for the same items, bargains become harder to find. Shopping wisely becomes more important. In this chapter, you learn bidding strategies that can maximize your chances of getting what you want at the price you want.

Getting What You Want

Internet auctions can be heart-pounding, exciting events. You can easily get carried away and make impulsive bids as the end of the auction approaches. Every time that you reload the eBay Web page, your Web browser retrieves new information from the auction site, including any bids since you last loaded the Web page. It's easy to get carried away in the excitement of the moment.

To avoid remorse when you have to actually *pay* for the item, however, you need to make sure that you bid wisely. To this end, the Internet offers you a virtual library full of data on countless types of consumer merchandise, from the latest high-tech gadgets to ancient antiquities. By using such resources, you can more readily place smart bids that you're not going to regret later.

Research the merchandise

In the traditional auction world, you can take advantage of the knowledge of experts that the auction houses hire to evaluate and appraise sale items, vouching for their authenticity. On eBay, however, you do most of the appraising yourself.

One of the best sources of sales information on the Internet is eBay's archive of past sales. You can search this database to determine what high bidders paid in the past for items similar to those on which you're considering bidding. To check out past sales records for a particular item, just follow these steps:

1. Click the **Search** link (see Figure 4-1) on the navigation bar at the top of any eBay page (including the home page) to access the eBay Search for Items page.

Figure 4-1:   The Search link.

| Search |

2. Scroll down to the Completed Auctions area near the bottom of the Find Items page.

3. Enter search terms in the text box to search titles. Select the Descending radio button if you want to check out the most recent auctions at the top of the list; select the Ascending radio button to check out the oldest auctions first.

4. Click the Search button. In a few seconds, a Search Result page appears. Scroll down the page to view the results of recent (or not-so-recent) auctions.

A search for Leica IIIC camera transactions that I conducted in May 1999 turned up 21 matches, some of which are as shown in Figure 4-2.

Figure 4-2: Use the Completed Auctions area of the Find Items page to find out what others bid on eBay for items similar to those you want to buy.

Item#	Item	Price	Bids	Ends
138264991	Leica IIIc with Summitar 50mm f2 with Hood **PIC**	$305.00	17	in 41 mins
138547865	Leica Ic, IIc, IIIc Camera Literature **PIC**	$10.00	1	08/04 15:49
138596091	LEITZ-LEICA IIIC Camera Case - Brown **PIC**	$15.50	6	08/04 17:18
139619614	Leica IIIc w/50mm f2 Summitar **PIC**	$132.50	5	08/06 18:50
139738265	LEICA CHROME Screw-In Body Cap IIIc IIIf IIIg	$14.95	0	08/06 22:50
140290587	Leica IIIc Screwmount Camera & 3 Lenses	$750.00	0	08/08 09:17
140610271	LEICA IIIC WITH 50 MM ELMAR, Nice Condition! **PIC**	$148.17	6	08/08 18:20

Don't take the prices that you see in the Price column on the Search Result page too seriously. The prices shown on the Search Result page may represent the high bids for an item, but they may not be *successful* bids because they may or may not have met the seller's reserve price. To determine whether anyone met the reserve price, click the Auction link.

The Completed Auction feature gives you information only about eBay sales during the last month or so, but these figures still provide you with a pretty good indication of the going market price for some highly valuable items.

You can also use the Completed Auction feature to get an idea of how much something is worth even if you don't plan to buy it right away — in other words, you can perform your own appraisals by looking up previous sales on eBay.

Bid with your head (not your heart)

Experienced bidders at traditional auction sales already know (or should know) not to let their emotions carry them away while bidding. Savvy bidders can use the extended time periods that online auctions involve to their advantage.

Auctions on eBay generally last three days or more, with a week being the most common duration. Because you know exactly when the sale ends, you have plenty of time to decide whether to bid and, if so, how much.

Before you bid on any item, make a dispassionate appraisal. Besides making your own online appraisals by searching eBay's database of past auctions, go to the local library and find price guides or antique guides that provide values for the merchandise in question. If you're looking for antiques or collectibles, keep the following criteria in mind before you click your mouse button to place your first bid:

■ **Historical importance:** An item's value often depends on its connection to a historical figure or event and how well-documented that connection is.

■ **Rarity:** The scarcity of an item (combined with beauty, condition, and other qualities) directly affects its value.

■ **Authenticity:** In the world of antiques, this criteria is one of the most important — one that you're best off leaving to the experts to determine by reading their detailed descriptions and viewing photos in guidebooks you can find at the local library and bookstores.

Tip

Consider following the example of some bidders who place a low initial bid early in a sale on the chance, however remote, that the seller may decide to end the sale early or that he receives no other bids (*and* if the initial bid meets any reserve price that has been set). In the case of a tie, the first bidder wins.

If you're looking for new merchandise, especially household appliances and computer-related items, check for price information on Web sites that gather current or recent sales prices for a wide range of products. These sites include PriceWatch, as shown in Figure 4-3, (`www.pricewatch.com`) and PriceScan (`www.pricescan.com`).

Figure 4-3: Sites such as PriceWatch gather retail prices for consumer goods so that shoppers can make comparisons.

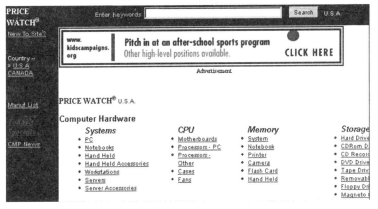

Bidding Strategies

Strategy can play an important role in Internet auction buying. A *bidding strategy* is a particular way to bid on an item to better your chances of winning the auction.

I describe the more common bidding strategies, as well as the pros and cons that help you decide which strategy to choose, in the following sections.

Proxy Bidding

One of your most important strategies on eBay and other auction sites involves using an automatic bidding system called *proxy bidding*. Such a system places bids for you without requiring you to actually be present online. The advantage of such a system is that you don't need to keep checking in with the auction to stay in the competition for an item.

One aspect of automatic bidding on eBay is the use of *proxy bids* to hold off challengers. In a proxy bid, you bid the maximum you're willing to pay for an item rather than the minimum increment. eBay records your maximum bid but keeps it secret until someone tries to outbid you. In the meantime, eBay takes the public step of placing only the minimum bid increment online for you.

For instance, if the current high bid is $25 and the bid increment is fifty cents, you can place a maximum proxy bid of $35 but the auction listing will only publicly display your high bid as $25.50. (That is, unless the current high bidder placed a maximum proxy bid before your bid. In that case, eBay will place your maximum bid in competition with the previous bidder's maximum bid; eBay will bid the previous bidder's maximum bid against yours by proxy, which is why it's called a *proxy* bid.) If your bid is higher than anyone else's previously placed proxy bid, the result is that any competitors for the item must beat your *maximum* bid — not the currently visible bid — to be the high bidder.

To make use of proxy bidding, you must specify a maximum bid amount that is far higher than either the current high bid. In effect, you're telling eBay to place the minimum high bid necessary for you to become the high bidder now but to keep your maximum high bid in reserve secretly. Then, if anyone outbids your current high bid, eBay automatically places a proxy bid for you, increasing your bid until reaching your maximum.

To specify a maximum bid that eBay places for you by proxy, if necessary, consider the example auction sale shown in Figure 4-4.

Figure 4-4: You can specify a maximum bid that eBay will make for you by proxy only if someone tries to outbid your current offer.

Current bid	**$65.00**
Bid increment	**$1.00**
Minimum bid	**$66.00**

Registration required. eBay requires registration in order to bid. Find out how to become a registered user. It's fast and it's **free**!

To finalize your bid, you will need to submit your User ID and Password in the next step — once you click on Review Bid.

`98.00` *Current minimum bid is 66.00* [review bid]

Enter your maximum bid
- Remember to type in **numbers only** and use a decimal point (.) when necessary. **Don't include a currency symbol ($) or thousand separator.** For example: 1000000.00

Someone may have already placed a maximum bid of, say, $44 for the item shown in Figure 4-4 *before* I place my own bid. (You can't tell whether anyone's placed such a bid; eBay keeps all proxy bids secret.) If so, my initial maximum bid of $98 results in a bid of $44.50 appearing on-screen. I've successfully outbid the other bidder's proxy bid.

Sniping

Sniping refers to the practice of placing a bid just a few minutes or seconds before an auction ends so that other bidders can't place a counter-offer. On sites such as eBay's, where auctions end exactly at the time specified by the seller, this strategy can help you win auctions. (Some Internet auction sites, such as Amazon.com Auctions, extend auctions so that bidders can place counter-offers if someone places a last-minute "snipe" bid.)

If you decide to snipe, you want to refrain from getting into the auction until the last few minutes. You just keep reloading your Web page to check on the progress of the auction. (On Microsoft Internet Explorer, you do so by choosing View↪Refresh or by pressing the F5 key. On Netscape Navigator, you choose View↪Reload or press Ctrl+R.)

You then place a bid just before the auction ends. You want to place a proxy bid that represents the absolute maximum amount you're willing to pay, because you have no idea whether the high bidder's currently posted bid is really the maximum he's willing to pay. Keep reloading the auction listing Web page to see whether anyone has counter-bid you at the last minute. If that happens, you can try to quickly enter a counter-bid if you have time. If no time is left, you're "outsniped."

Sniping isn't illegal, but it is a somewhat devious way of bidding and one that may well arouse the ire of the competing bidders you defeat at the last minute. Nevertheless, it's a common practice — and it works. Sniping can, however, backfire if anything unexpected happens at the critical moment — your computer crashes, your Internet connection fails to work, the auction service fails to respond, or your modem starts to crawl slowly.

Bid Increments

In order to use any of the preceding bid strategies effectively, it's important to understand *bid increments*. A bid increment is a minimum amount by which bids must increase. To be the high bidder, a shopper must place a bid at least 50 cents higher than the current high bid.

Bid increments depend on the current high bid on the item. The increment increases automatically as bids increase. When the high bid moves from $99 to $105, for instance, the increment jumps from $1 to $2.50.

Table 4-1 illustrates how the increments increase as the sale price increases. (All prices are in U.S. dollars. The increments are subject to change; for the current values, go to **Help** ☞ Glossary Terms ☞ Bid Increment.)

Table 4-1: eBay Bid Increments

Current Bid	Bid Increment
.01–.99	.05
1.00–4.99	.25
5.00–24.99	.50
25.00–99.99	1.00
100.00–249.99	2.50
250.00–499.99	5.00
500.00–999.99	10.00
1000.00–2499.99	25.00
2500.00–4999.99	50.00
5000.00 and up	100.00

Bidding in Reserve Auctions

A *reserve price* is the lowest price at which a seller is willing to sell an item. For a bidder to win the auction, he must make not only the highest bid, but the bid must also meet or exceed the reserve price that the seller set. If no one meets the reserve price, neither the seller nor the high bidder is under any obligation to complete the deal. The reserve price remains hidden from bidders until someone places a bid that meets or exceeds that amount.

Not all eBay auctions use a reserve price; you can tell whether a seller's specified one for an item by looking at the current high bid on the auction page. (That is, the page where the item for auction is described in detail and the seller and high bidder are identified.) If you see the words `Reserve not yet met` next to the amount of the high bid, you know that the seller set a reserve price and that it's higher than the current high bid.

If you see the words `Reserve met` next to the amount of the high bid, you know that the current high bid meets or exceeds the seller's reserve price and the item is going to sell at that amount unless someone else places a higher bid before the sale ends. If you don't see either phrase next to the amount of the high bid, you know that the item carries no reserve price.

One bidding strategy to use for auctions with reserve prices is to bid a round amount, such as $50, $100, $150, and so on, in an attempt to discover the reserve price. (A round amount is useful because sellers often specify a round amount as the reserve price.) Note what the current high bid is — and bid the next round number higher than that if it's not near your own maximum.

The round amount bidding strategy can help you determine whether the item is worth bidding on or is too expensive for you. If, for example, you're interested in an item that carries a reserve price and you're willing to pay only $100 for it, bid $100. If the words *Reserve not yet met* continue to appear after your high bid shows up on the page, you know that the reserve is higher than you want, at which point you can continue shopping for a similar item in your price range. And if you bid significantly higher than the reserve amount, you are stuck with the bid.

If the high bidder doesn't meet the seller's reserve price, the two can communicate by e-mail or over the phone (if they decide to trade phone numbers) and negotiate a compromise price.

Participating in Dutch Auctions

A *Dutch auction* differs dramatically from the more common eBay auctions in which a single winner pays the highest price. Sellers use Dutch auctions when they have multiple versions of the same item to sell. In a Dutch auction, everyone pays the same price, which is the same as the *lowest qualifying* bid.

In a Dutch auction, the seller specifies a minimum bid. Each bidder makes a bid and specifies the number of items that he or she wants. If all the bids are the same, then the bidders who bid earliest get first dibs on the items.

However, if someone makes a higher bid for an item, that person gets dibs over every lower bidder, even though higher bidders end up paying the same amount as the lowest qualifying bidder. If the demand for an item outstrips supply, the lowest bidders may be outbid by higher bidders and the lowest qualifying bid may go up. In effect, placing a higher bid means "I'm willing to pay more if I have to."

The strategy to use in making Dutch bids is to avoid being the low bidder. The problem with being the low bidder before the auction ends is that the low bidder is "on the bubble." You can easily be outbid by someone else placing a last-minute bid that's a little higher than your bid. Instead, bid at the last minute and place a bid that makes you the second-lowest bidder. Just make sure that you're in the winner's circle without being in the low bid position.

You can find eBay's explanation of how Dutch auctions work at `pages.ebay.com/aw/help/help-faq-format.html`. The eBay Underground FAQ page also contains a good explanation of this strategy (at `http://www.frii.com/~afs/ebay`).

CHAPTER 5

PROTECTING YOURSELF AGAINST FRAUD

IN THIS CHAPTER

- Researching traders and/or merchandise
- Finding places to turn in case of trouble
- Insuring your transaction
- Maintaining your privacy online

Whether you're a buyer or seller, your auction transactions on eBay are likely to proceed smoothly. The people you do business with will probably prove themselves to be trustworthy, and you'll likely find the outcome of the sale pleasing. Many users of eBay's person-to-person auctions, however, aren't professional businesspeople, and a few are even dishonest.

Whether because of fraudulent or careless behavior, some participants may not honor their commitments. The most common problems occur if buyers submit winning bids and then disappear without submitting payment or sellers accept payment but never ship what they sold.

In this chapter, which concerns both buyers and sellers, you learn how to minimize your chances of being involved in unsuccessful transactions. Nobody can guarantee 100-percent satisfaction in each and every sale, but you can usually protect yourself through preparation and common sense.

Preventing Trouble through Research

You can increase your odds of satisfaction with the results of an online transaction by arming yourself with knowledge before the sale takes place. If you're a buyer, you need to research the merchandise that you want to purchase and to look into the seller's background If you're a seller, you need to make price comparisons and obtain sales data so that you can set fair prices and write accurate descriptions. See Chapter 3 for suggestions on how to do research on eBay sales using eBay's databases.

eBay provides its members with several ways to communicate and conduct research before, during, and after a sale. Your task is to use the tools that eBay provides so that you feel informed and sure of what to do at critical moments in a transaction, such as when the seller publishes the listing, when the buyer bids, when the sale closes, and when you complete the deal.

Communicating with buyers and sellers

The best way to avoid getting swindled, cheated, or fooled by a seller or a buyer is to establish some sort of personal contact with the other person so that you know something about him first.

Although you may never meet face to face, you can use e-mail to establish close personal communication so that you can judge the other party's responsiveness and knowledge of the material up for auction. (I've received positive feedback myself for e-mail inquiries that I've sent to sellers before placing any bids. An example of such an initial contact is shown in Figure 5-1.)

Figure 5-1: Use e-mail to make contact, ask questions, and judge someone's reliability.

> **Subject: Question re Astoria espresso machine**
> **Date:** Wed, 04 Aug 1999 06:58:54 -0500
> **From:** Greg Holden <gholden@interaccess.com>
> **Organization:** InterAccess, Chicagoland's Full-Service Internet Provider
> **To:**
>
> Dear mswenson,
>
> I am very interested in the espresso machine you are auctioning. It would be a sizeable investment for me, so I would like to know what it looks like. Is the one you are selling the same as one of the machines depicted on the following Web page:
>
> http://
>
> Also, are you required to use tap water with this machine, or is plain old tap water OK?
>
> Thanks very much,
>
> Greg Holden

Feel free to go beyond the simple facts of payment methods and delivery addresses and to engage the seller in conversation about things she collects or purchases at auction herself. Ask about any flaws or special features in the item you're considering. Ask how old the object is and where she obtained it. And find out whether the seller's actually used the item herself. The detail and tone of the responses you get should give you, at the very least, a rough idea of whether you can safely do business with the seller.

If you're a seller and you're reluctant to deal with people who live hundreds or even thousands of miles from you, sell only to buyers who live in your own geographical area. A good way to let people know up front about this preference is to specify your policy in your auction listing. Doing so narrows your sales options, but it may provide you with peace of mind.

On occasion, sellers who auction off heavy or bulky items (such as exercise equipment) state that they're willing to deal only with people who live close enough to pick up the merchandise in person, which saves them the time and trouble of packing and shipping the object.

Investigating feedback

The feedback system that I describe in Chapter 7 is your first resource for looking into previous transactions of other buyers and sellers. One way to reduce your chances of getting cheated by a seller is to make sure that you deal only with individuals who've accumulated a substantial number of positive comments from previous buyers. Such feedback indicates that the seller's been auctioning online for a considerable amount of time and is more likely, therefore, to be trustworthy.

If you're a seller, take a look into the high bidder's background after the sale's over, either by clicking the feedback rating number in parentheses next to his User ID or by checking out the Feedback Forum page. (See the information about the Feedback Forum in Chapter 7.) You can't control who's going to win your auction, but you can make yourself aware of any previous problem with transactions involving that buyer.

Pricing and researching merchandise

If you trade at auction, whether as buyer or seller, researching what's on the virtual block is every bit as important as knowing who's on the other end of the transaction. If you're selling, it pays to know how valuable your item is and what features you can describe that will attract prospective buyers

Although the Internet provides an immediate form of exchange, you still want to avoid rushing into a purchase. Before bidding, you need to identify what a fair price is for any item up for auction as well as determine what features are desirable in such an item. Luckily for both buyers and sellers, eBay opens its archives of past auctions to anyone who wants to know what certain objects sold for in the past. See Chapter 4 for instructions on how to uncover such data.

The eBay Verified User program

One way to make sure that the person with whom you're dealing is legitimate is to deal only with verified eBay users. eBay is currently working a new Verified eBay User program that can help you in doing so. You can find more information about this new program by browsing to **Help** ☞ **Basics** on the navigation bar and then clicking the <u>Verified eBay User</u> hyperlink under the FAQ heading, as shown in Figure 5-2.

Figure 5-2: The eBay Verified User FAQ.

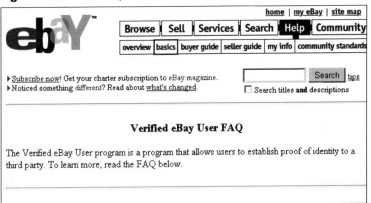

The program was originally to start in March 1999 but hasn't yet begun as the time of this writing. After the program's available, you can register yourself as a verified user for six months for $5/month. A third-party service, Equifax, Inc. (at www.equifax.com), handles the verification and also performs credit checks for individuals or businesses. The system alerts you if someone's phone number doesn't match his zip code, or if the address he supplies is, for example, a mail-receiving service or a prison.

Verifying a user's identity outside eBay

Although an eBay user must submit a username and password (as well as an address and other information) during the registration process, as of this writing, you have no way to guarantee the authenticity of that information. Just as can happen in the real world, nothing prevents anyone from submitting stolen credit card information online. At presstime, eBay is taking steps to verify the identity of its registered users.

You can, however, take your own measures to prevent fraud. If a first-time seller is offering the item that you want to bid on, you can search online for evidence that the seller really is whom he claims to be.

Nothing's necessarily wrong with someone having more than one registered username at an auction service such as eBay. eBay, in fact, permits sellers to submit two registered names.

One scam that crops up on eBay and other services is that of the phantom seller — someone who registers under a fictitious name, scams some hapless customer, and after receiving negative feedback, simply reregisters to continue conducting scams under a different name. The safest strategy is to only bid on items being offered by established sellers who have accumulated positive feedback.

If you're interested in items that less-established sellers are offering, make sure that you can independently verify the person's company, phone, address, and so on before you bid on their merchandise. Doing so at least minimizes, if not eliminates, the likelihood of fraud. You can go about this in a couple of ways:

■ **Ask them outright for a full name and address.** Ask them for this information in an e-mail. A more subtle option is to send an e-mail message asking about the item for sale; look for a full name or, better yet, a link to a Web page or other biographical information in the seller's signature file, if there is one.

■ **Look up the person on an Internet White Pages service.** By doing so, you can at least verify that the person lives at their address. Yahoo! People (at `people. yahoo.com`) and Switchboard (at `www.switch board.com`) are good places to start. Switchboard is actually an Internet phone book" service, as shown in Figure 5-3.

Certifying your own identity

Another way to provide your fellow traders with a measure of security that you're who you say you are is to obtain an electronic form of identification known as a *Digital ID*, or *personal certificate*.

Figure 5-3: You can try to verify someone's eBay user information by using an independent "white pages" Web site such as this one.

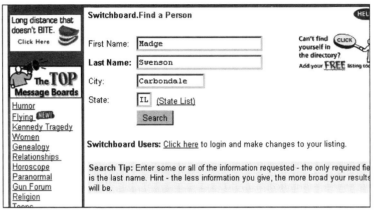

A Digital ID is a computer document that uses a form of encryption known as *public/private key security* to protect secure information that you transmit on the Internet. This document includes a *public key*, which is a very long series of numbers and characters that a mathematical formula known as an *algorithm* generates. A *private key*, which you keep on your computer and obtain at the time that you apply for the certificate, accompanies your public key. If you obtain a Digital ID, a company known as *a certification authority* thereby certifies your identity.

You can obtain a trial version of a Digital ID for free for 60 days or buy one for an annual fee of $14.95 at the VeriSign Web site (www.verisign.com). (This site is a good place to find some user-friendly information about how public/private key encryption works, by the way.) Businesses that engage in electronic commerce are the main users of such IDs, but they're available to individuals as well.

Finding Help in Case You Need It

Customer service is an essential feature of any business, but it's especially important on the Internet, where technology is relatively new and often confusing for some users. eBay gives you a wide range of options to employ if you end up in a disagreement that you can't resolve or need to report a suspected case of fraud. You can turn to these resources whenever your attempts to "talk out" a problem don't seem to work.

eBay's SafeHarbor

eBay calls its customer service area *SafeHarbor*. You can access it directly at `pages.ebay.com/aw/safeharbor-index.html`. If you're unsuccessful in resolving a disagreement or you simply can't locate a buyer or seller who may have cheated you, involve eBay's SafeHarbor Investigations service on your behalf.

You start by locating any e-mail messages that relate to the transaction that you need SafeHarbor to investigate — for example, any notifications from eBay about bids or about the end of the auction, any communications you received from the other person involved, and any you sent to that person.

Then, armed with this information, you can go directly to the SafeHarbor Investigations page (at `pages.ebay.com/aw/safeharbor-investigates.html`), as shown in Figure 5-4. Read the definitions of the kinds of offenses that SafeHarbor investigates and see whether your situation falls into any of those categories. if they don't, you need to contact one of the resources listed later in this chapter in the section "Other online resources."

Compose an e-mail message describing your case and send it to SafeHarbor at `safeharbor@ebay.com`. Paste the text of the e-mails that relate to your case into the body of the message. SafeHarbor then investigates the incident and takes disciplinary action if necessary.

Be prepared to send an inquiry to `safeharbor@ebay.com` to find out the results of the investigation.

Figure 5-4: This area of eBay's SafeHarbor site is the place to turn if you need eBay to investigate a problem on your behalf.

Other eBay problem-solvers

SafeHarbor is probably the first place that you want to turn if you think you've been defrauded. But if SafeHarbor decides not to investigate or doesn't take action you think is warranted, you have other options as well, as the following list describes:

■ **Fraud Reporting System:** eBay's Fraud Reporting System staff (at `pages.ebay.com/aw/frs-down.html`) can try to contact the offender and, if unsuccessful, possibly remove the person from the eBay system.

■ **Mediation:** If eBay's SafeHarborfraud-resolution services aren't working and you're still in contact with the seller, you can try a professional mediator. At this writing, eBay is developing a program with the Online Ombuds Office of the University of Massachusetts, but the program isn't up and running yet. Check its status at `pages.ebay.com/aw/safeharbor-mediation.html`.

■ **Got a Question?** Clicking the link <u>Help</u> at the top of any page on the eBay Web site takes you to the eBay Help: Starting Point page. If you have a question that needs immediate attention, scroll down to the <u>Got a Question?</u> link at the bottom of this page. This link takes you to the eBay Help: Support page, which includes links to eBay's Q-and-A and other support message boards.

■ **The Emergency Contact message board.** This message board is a forum where you can post messages to users you need to reach in a hurry but for whom you don't have phone or e-mail contact information. To access this board, go to the eBay News & Chat page (at `pages.ebay.com/aw/newschat.html`) and click the <u>Emergency Contact</u> link.

Other online resources

Realizing that online auctions are not only popular but also occasionally fraught with risk, a growing number of agencies offer reporting systems for handling complaints. The following list describes some places that you can visit for assistance or information:

■ **The U.S. Post Office:** If you think you've been victimized by mail fraud, call the U.S. Post Office's Crime Hot Line at (800) 654-8896.

■ **The National Fraud Information Center:** The NFIC also maintains a toll-free hot line that you can call at 1-800-876-7060 as well as its own Web site (www.fraud.org), shown in Figure 5-5.

■ **The Web Police:** You can file a report on the Web Police's page (at www.Web-Police.org) and add your information to its database of Internet crime cases.

Figure 5-5: The NFIC can forward your complaint to the appropriate government agency for action.

■ **Internet ScamBusters:** The Internet ScamBusters' Web page (at www.scambusters.org/Scambusters21.html) contains more tips and resources for victims of fraud, including the page "What to Do If You Get Scammed."

■ **The Better Business Bureau:** If you believe you have been defrauded by a seller who operates his or her own business, you can also you file a complaint online with the Better Business Bureau (at www.bbb.org). The BBB attempts to facilitate communication between the seller's company and you.

Turning to an agency outside of eBay can often intimidate a buyer or seller into cooperating with you after the person receives notification from the agency that an investigation is underway. The first two organizations in the preceding list are especially good examples.

Insuring Your Transaction through eBay

One of the best consumer features that credit card companies offer is insurance in case that the merchandise you purchase with the card gets stolen, lost, or damaged. eBay is trying to provide insurance to its member as well. eBay recently set up a program with the insurance carrier Lloyd's of London.

The program, which is available to all eBay users in good standing, covers items listed on eBay that you bought on or after March 1, 1999. Coverage for your purchases extends up to $200, minus a $25 deductible.

To qualify for coverage, the final value of the item must be more than $25, and both buyer and seller must be in good standing at eBay. (Both users must have positive feedback ratings; see Chapter 7 for more information on eBay's Feedback system.)

If you feel that you have been defrauded and want to file an insurance claim, you must fill out the eBay Fraud Reporting and Insurance Claim form (from the eBay home page, scroll to the bottom of the page and click on SafeHarbor ☞ Insurance ☞ Fraud Reporting Process) within 30 days of the auction's close. After you do so, the Fraud Reporting System contacts the seller, informing him that you filed a complaint. If you haven't solved the problem within 30 days, you can return to the Fraud Reporting System to file or delete your complaint.

If you file the Fraud Reporting and Insurance Claim Form and are eligible, you then receive information on obtaining insurance. If you delete your complaint, your complaint against the other user is removed.

By filling out the form mentioned above, your insurance claim is sent in to Lloyd's claim administrators. After you file a claim, Lloyd's claim administrators contact you within 45 days to tell you the results of their investigation.

CHAPTER 6

COMPLETING THE TRANSACTION

IN THIS CHAPTER

- Paying for long-distance auction purchases
- Making sure that you receive payment for what you sell
- Shipping options that help you track the goods
- Insuring your auction purchase

The action that occurs after the eBay sale is complete often carries the greatest uncertainty for both buyers and sellers. Both you and the other party must now make good on your commitments. Not all potential difficulties arise as a result of fraud. Packages can become lost during the shipment process, for example, or banks can take a long time in clearing checks.

An agreement involving eBay and two shipping companies now streamlines the process of sending auction merchandise from buyer to seller. Escrow services also take much of the anxiety out of transferring funds for payment. In this chapter, you learn how to use these and other resources for completing your auction transaction with more success and less stress.

Selecting a Payment Option

If you purchase something in a retail store, payment is simple: You hand over your check, cash, or credit card to the salesperson, and then you walk away with your merchandise.

Even phone purchases involve a certain measure of security, because you're giving your credit card information directly to a catalog or retail store employee over the phone.

If you don't make payment by phone or in person, however, the procedure seems much less straightforward. But eBay also gives you options for increasing the security of your online transactions through eBay as well, either as a buyer or as a seller, as I explain in the following sections.

Cashier's checks and money orders

Cashier's checks and money orders are usually the most popular forms of payment on auction sites. In fact, if you're a seller filling out eBay's form for listing a new sales item, cashier's checks and money orders are the first items that you check off (see Figure 6-1). You can select other forms of payment or shipping options as well by clicking the appropriate check boxes on the form. If you do so, text appears in your auction description that tells prospective bidders about your preferred forms or payment or shipping.

Figure 6-1: The majority of eBay sellers accept cashier's checks and money orders.

Payment Methods Choose all that you will accept	☐ Money Order/Cashiers Check	☐ Personal Check	☐ Visa/MasterCard
	☐ COD (collect on delivery)	☐ On-line Escrow	☐ American Express
	☑ See Item Description	☐ Other	☐ Discover
Where will you ship?	⦿ Ship to Seller's Country Only see tips	○ Will Ship Internationally	
Who pays for shipping?	☐ Seller Pays Shipping	☐ Buyer Pays Fixed Amount	
	☐ Buyer Pays Actual Shipping Cost	☑ See Item Description	

Cashier's checks and money orders are popular because they're guaranteed not to bounce — you've already shelled out the cash to pay for them. You must visit a bank or a post office to obtain them, however, and you usually must pay a service charge as well.

Sending cash through the mail is never smart. If a buyer or seller suggests that you do so, politely decline and request an alternative method.

Sellers who receive a money order can deposit it and then send the merchandise immediately. Cashier's checks, on the other hand, can take several days to clear, so most sellers delay shipment until they receive the actual payment.

If you're high bidder on an item that an overseas seller is offering, get your money order from a U.S. bank rather than from the U.S. Post Office. Sometimes overseas users can't cash postal money orders and in general have a much easier time with money orders drawn on U.S. bank accounts.

Most sellers relish the security of receiving a tangible piece of certified paper. Some online companies, however, are trying to come up with virtual forms of payment such as electronic cash, but these aren't widely used. Credit card payments online are much more widespread and easy to use, as described in the following section.

Credit card payments

Occasionally, you see an eBay auction listing that includes credit cards among its payment options (see Figure 6-2). Sometimes, the seller even includes credit card logos as part of the listing.

Credit cards simplify auction payments in the following ways:

■ **Efficiency:** You can make your payment by phone, fax, or e-mail and it's processed in minutes.

■ **Security:** The seller doesn't need to worry about a check clearing, and some cards insure the buyer against loss as well.

Figure 6-2:   Some (but by no means all) auction sellers accept credit card payments for eBay transactions.

Payment	Visa/MasterCard, American Express, Discover, Money Order/Cashiers Checks, Personal Checks, Online escrow
Shipping	Buyer pays actual shipping charges, Seller ships internationally

Seller assumes all responsibility for listing this item. You should contact the seller to resolve any questions before bidding. Currency is dollar ($) unless otherwise noted.

Description

new rolex tudor tiger stainless chronograph WITH BLANK PAPERS AND ALL THE BOXES ETC., with a PORCELAIN WHITE FACE and black MARKERS AND HANDS, SILVER BEZEL, has rolEx BLACK leather deployment band, all the papers boxes ets, runs fine , thanks, ralph

The downside is that many buyers are reluctant to give a credit card number to someone whose identity they can't verify. To accept credit cards, sellers must apply to a bank for a merchant account. This process can take several weeks. After a seller obtains the account, he needs to take the following two additional actions:

■ **Processing:** Instead of handing over a check for processing, the seller needs to transmit sales information to a financial institution. This process requires some extra work, although software such as Authorizer (at www.atomic-software.com) can help streamline the process.

■ **Verification:** A smart seller at the very least compares the shipping address that the buyer provides to the address associated with the credit card as a way of checking that the buyer's not using a stolen credit card number. You do the verification by contacting a credit card verification company like Otagon Technology Group (www.otginc.com) or by using a program such as Authorizer by Atomic Software.

Credit card merchant accounts are becoming easier for individual sellers and small businesses to obtain, although doing so can still prove a time-consuming process. Yahoo! offers a Web page full of financial institutions to which you can apply if you're a seller or own your own business. To check it out, point your browser to Yahoo!'s home page (www.yahoo.com) and then click **Business_and_Economy** ☞ Companies ☞ Financial Services ☞ Transaction Clearing ☞ Credit Card Merchant Services. Wells Fargo Bank (at www.wellsfargo.com) also provides you with a good overview of the requirements for obtaining a merchant account.

Sellers on eBay who can accept credit card payments do enjoy certain advantages. But many sellers go through hundreds of successful transactions without such payments.

Even if you don't have your own merchant account, you can accept credit card payments from a high bidder if you use an escrow service to handle the payment and shipping, as I describe in the following section.

Using Escrow Services

Frustrated auction buyers and sellers often make such comments as "Why didn't I think of that before?" after they learn about online escrow services and how such services can ensure successful transactions.

An *escrow service* is a business that functions as an intermediary between someone who provides goods or services and someone who pays money in exchange. (The word *escrow* refers to a bond or agreement between two parties to do something — usually *pay* something — in exchange for goods or services; the "something" is usually held by a third party until the supplier delivers the goods or renders the services.)

Getting help from an escrow service

An escrow service protects both auction buyers and sellers by holding the buyer's money until he confirms that the product he receives matches what the seller described. For an example, see Internet Clearing Corporation (see Figure 6-3). If the item doesn't meet with the buyer's approval (or if the buyer never receives it), the escrow company refunds the buyer's money. The escrow company charges a fee for these services, and using these services does add some steps to the overall process.

Figure 6-3: Escrow companies act as intermediaries in personal transactions on the Internet, but each has different fees and procedures.

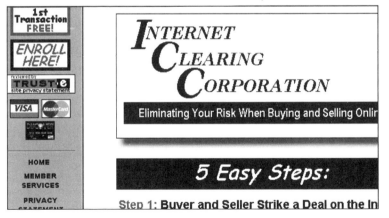

Although many sellers have concerns about the extra bureaucratic "layer" escrow services bring to the transaction, the escrow system offers certain benefits to sellers as well. By using the security of an escrow service, for example, a seller can ship the merchandise the same day that the auction closes and still be confident of receiving payment. And the escrow service tracks any packages sellers ship to buyers.

For buyers, escrow services bring flexibility to the transaction. They make credit card transactions feasible for individuals and are good to use for overseas transactions that can take extra time and involve currency exchange. Finally, the escrow company commonly passes its charges on to the buyer, while the seller pays only the shipping fees.

Comparing escrow services

As do auction houses, all escrow services have their own fees and procedures. You always want to compare the prices and requirements of different companies to make sure that a service fits your particular needs.

Following are a few of the differences between three of the prominent online escrow companies:

- **Internet Clearing Corporation** requires the buyer to provide sales data to the escrow service, in contrast to iEscrow (see the following list item). Internet Clearing Corporation also has a fax service that makes faxing sales information to the service especially easy for users who're wary of filling out and submitting data via Web page forms.

  By using Internet Clearing Corporation, the seller receives payment immediately on shipping an item instead of needing to wait until the buyer inspects and approves it. The buyer can still return the item by the end of the following business day, however, and get a refund. Internet Clearing Corporation holds the purchase money until the item is approved or rejected. If rejected, the buyer will get the purchase price refunded (less the transaction fee) after the seller receives the item back from the buyer.

- **iEscrow** permits either buyer or seller to provide information about what is being sold, what the sale price is, and so on. iEscrow also requires sellers to ship items by using a package-tracking service, such as that of the U.S. Postal Service. Other services don't specify such a requirement but require you to use FedEx or United Parcel Service (UPS) and *not* the U.S. Postal Service.

- **SecureTrades** offers a merchandise holding option: The seller ships the merchandise to SecureTrades rather than to the buyer. SecureTrades then ships the goods so that the buyer is certain that he receives something. Secure-Trades accepts only checks or money orders, however, and not credit cards.

Shopping around to compare prices among escrow services usually pays off in the long run, just as it does in searching for auction merchandise to purchase. Table 6-1 briefly summarizes the user fees that the four escrow services that I mention in the preceding list charge. (These fees are subject to change; check the individual Web sites for the most up-to-date information.)

Table 6-1:   Internet Escrow Service Fees and Regulations

Service	URL	Fee for $100	Fee for $1,000	Remarks
iEscrow	www. iescrow. com	$6	$30	Either buyer or seller can initiate transaction.

(continued)

Table 6-1: **Internet Escrow Service Fees and Regulations *(continued)***

Service	URL	Fee for $100	Fee for $1,000	Remarks
Internet Clearing Corporation	www. internet clearing. com	$1.50 both buyer and seller.	$15 both buyer and seller.	First transaction free for purchases of up to $1,000. No credit card purchases for transactions of $5,000 or more.
Secure Trades	secure trades. com	$5	$50	Merchandise Holding option requires higher fees; see Web site.
TradeSafe	www. tradesafe. com	$5	$50	

Most auction buyers and sellers who use escrow services end up glad that they did. The main problem is usually just getting them to try out such a service in the first place. (Although another problem is making sure that both participants register with the same service. Registration is generally a matter of filling out an online form; it's free and only takes a few minutes.) Don't wait until you have a bad transaction before trying out these services.

Shipping and Package-Tracking

All the precautions that you take in regard to sellers, bids, and payment methods may prove useless if the merchandise is lost or incurs damage during shipping. Strictly speaking, at this stage, you're in the hands of the shipper, who must make sure that merchandise travels safely from seller to buyer. You can, however, protect yourself by observing the simple procedures that I outline in the following sections.

Looking up shipping costs

Shipping costs can be a shock and a source of disagreement that sours an otherwise smooth purchase. Smart sellers weigh their merchandise beforehand and estimate the shipping cost with reasonable accuracy. They can then either include the estimate in the auction description itself or provide the high bidder(s) with the correct information after the sale.

Some online resources can take the guesswork out of shipping costs. For materials you're sending via the U.S. Postal Service, you can estimate the cost by using the USPS International Rate Calculator (at `ircalc.usps.gov`).

Tracking your package

Virtually all the major shipping services enable you to track your packages online. Most provide you with a tracking number, and even those that don't can tell you with reasonable certainly how long a package takes to get from origin to destination so that you can determine whether one's overdue or look out for the package when it is supposed to arrive. Tracking numbers, especially, serve as an anxiety reliever for both buyer and seller (but primarily for the buyer) if merchandise seems to be taking too long in shipping. Shipping companies protect themselves by limiting their liability if a package is late or lost; read each company's service guide before you ship so you know what you're getting into.

The One-Stop Parcel Tracking Web site (at `www.upgradecity.com/tracking.htm`) enables you to track a package with any of seven major shipping organizations, including the U.S. Postal Service, as shown in Figure 6-4. Check out the Resource Center at the back of this book for a list of shipping services' Web sites, where you can enter your tracking number and get information about a package's whereabouts within seconds.

Insuring your investment

If you want to protect purchases that are especially high in value or precious for other reasons, ask the seller to insure it and tell the seller that you (the buyer) will pay a few extra dollars for protection. Insurance adds to the eventual purchase price, but for special items, it's worth the extra peace of mind.

Figure 6-4:   Make sure that you choose a shipping method that enables you to track a package at a site such as this one.

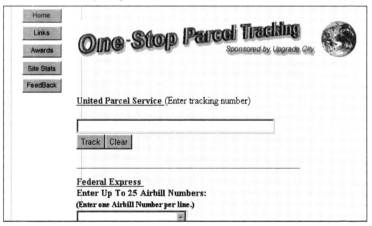

Respecting the 30-day rule

You can always cite an important law known as the *Mail or Telephone Order Rule* (commonly called the "30-Day Rule") that the U.S. Federal Trade Commission adopted in 1975 should you experience long delays in receiving what you purchase online from a seller.

The rule states that, if you order merchandise by mail or phone, whether from a traditional retail store or via the Internet, you must receive what you buy by the time that the seller indicates. If he specifies no specific delivery period, the seller must ship the merchandise to you no later than 30 days after you place your order. If you don't receive the item shortly after that 30-day period, you can cancel your order and receive a refund.

CHAPTER 7

JOINING THE EBAY COMMUNITY

IN THIS CHAPTER

- Using the feedback system
- Connecting with fellow traders at the Cafe
- Uncovering secrets about life on eBay
- Giving back through charity auctions

One of the things that makes eBay exceptional, both among Internet auction services and commercial Web sites in general, is the loyalty of its user community. A study released in early 1999 by the Internet measurement service Nielsen/NetRatings indicated that the average eBay user spends more than an hour on the site during a typical visit. This amount is far beyond the usual time (10–20 minutes) spent on most other Web sites.

What inspires such loyalty? The ever-changing content and the lure of good deals is certainly one factor. Another is the emphasis that eBay places on community-building among its members. eBay enables its customers to deal with one another not only as buyers and sellers but also as friends and colleagues. Community-building venues such as the eBay Cafe, eBay Life, and the Feedback Forum can help you learn about online auctions from the insiders who use them on a daily basis.

Giving Feedback on Buyers and Sellers

Feedback refers to comments that buyers and sellers register about one another on eBay. Customers type evaluations (pro or con) into an online form. eBay then posts them on its site along with accumulated reports from other users.

The feedback may stay online for weeks or months, and the list of positive and negative remarks may influence others who're deciding whether to do business with a particular person. Feedback is a part of eBay life that regular users take very seriously; leaving feedback for others and accumulating positive feedback yourself is essential for playing the "game" right.

The feedback rating appears in parentheses next to a person's User ID, which appears right next to the Seller heading near the top of the auction listing. The rating rises and falls according to the formula shown in Table 7-1.

Table 7-1:   Feedback and Its Effects

Type of Comment	Effect on User's Feedback Rating
Positive	Adds one point (+1) to the user's total.
Neutral	No effect (0) on the user's total.
Negative	Subtracts one point (-1) from the user's total.

Users with high feedback numbers get stars next to their names in their User IDs that reflect the amount of positive feedback they've accumulated. eBay's *Star ratings system* encourages users to keep getting positive comments over the course of hundreds or even thousands of transactions.

The color of the star represents the number of positive comments that user has received. A page that functions as a key to the Star system tells what each color means. To view this page, click the star next to a user's name.

Viewing feedback

To start using eBay's feedback system, you want to view the types of comments (positive, negative, or neutral, as mentioned in Table 7-1 above) that users leave for one another in the eBay Feedback Forum.

The easiest way to access the feedback rating and view the feedback comments left in the Feedback Forum for an individual user is to click on the number in parentheses next to the individual's User ID. For instance, if you see gholden@interaccess.com (6) next to the Seller or Bidder line on the auction listing page, click on the number 6. Your browser will access the individual's page in the Feedback Forum and you can view the feedback instantly.

If you already know the User ID of an individual (if you have written it down, for instance), you can access the feedback in a different way, by following these steps. (If you haven't written the User ID down, copied it to the Clipboard, or otherwise recorded it, you'll need to revisit an auction page where the individual is either selling or bidding on something, and either record the User ID or simply click on the feedback number in parentheses next to the User ID, as described above.

1. Access the eBay Feedback Forum Web page from the navigation bar by clicking **Services** ☞ **feedback forum**.

2. Click the <u>See Feedback about an eBay user</u> link. You connect to the See the Feedback Profile of an eBay User page.

3. Enter the eBay User ID of the individual you want to research into the User ID text box. You must spell the User ID correctly, although the name you enter isn't case-sensitive (that is, it doesn't matter if you get the capital and small letters perfect; just spell the name correctly). Click the Submit button and the Feedback Profile for *[User ID]* page appears, displaying the user's feedback rating (see Figure 7-1).

Figure 7-1:   A user's Feedback Profile contains comments that fellow eBay members leave.

Overall profile makeup		
6 positives. 5 are from unique users and count toward the final rating.		
0 neutrals. 0 are from users no longer registered.		
0 negatives. 0 are from unique users and count toward the final rating.		

eb Y ID card gholden@interaccess.com
(5)

Summary of Most Recent Comments

	Past 7 days	Past month	Past 6 mo.
Positive	0	0	1
Neutral	0	0	0
Negative	0	0	0
Total	**0**	**0**	**1**

Auctions by gholden@interaccess.com

To make sure that you enter another user's User ID correctly, look for it whenever you find a Web page or get an e-mail message from the person. Then highlight the username by dragging your cursor across the name (while holding the left mouse button). Press Ctrl+C (or ⌘-C on a Mac) to copy the name to your computer's Clipboard. Then you can paste it into the User ID text box by pressing Ctrl+V (or ⌘-V on a Mac).

4. Scroll down the page to read specific comments left for this user.

Another way to view a user's feedback profile is to click the hyperlinked number in parentheses next to the user's name which appears right next to the Seller heading near the top of the auction listing. In Figure 7-1, for example, you click the hyperlinked number (5) next to the User ID gholden@interaccess.com. (Clicking the hyperlinked User ID itself enables you to access the use's e-mail address and a history record indicating how long the user's been registered with eBay.)

Posting feedback

In order to build good readability and generate a good reputation so eBay users will want to do business with you, it's just as important to leave useful, specific feedback about someone as it is to uncover what comments others have left about you or someone. Courteous, brief, yet specific and fair comments make you look good and contribute to the feedback system as a whole.

To leave feedback about a buyer or seller, follow these steps:

1. Look up the user's feedback profile as described in the preceding section. You can also click either the <u>for seller</u> or <u>for buyer</u> hyperlink beneath the Leave Feedback icon at the left side of an auction-listing page.

2. Scroll down the Feedback Profile for *[User ID]* page and click the <u>leave feedback</u> hyperlink. The Leave Feedback about an eBay User page appears, as shown in Figure 7-2.

You can also access the Leave Feedback about an eBay User page directly. Visit the main Feedback Forum page (click Services ☞ feedback forum on the navigation bar) and then click the <u>Leave Feedback about an eBay user</u> link. In this case, you have to enter the user's ID in the space.

Figure 7-2:   Enter your feedback on this page.

Leave Feedback about an eBay User

Your registered User ID

Your password

User ID of person who you are commenting on

Item number (include if you want to relate the comment to a transaction)

You are responsible for your own words.

Your comments will be attributed with your name and the date. eBay cannot take responsibility for the comments you post here, and you should be careful about making comments that could be libelous or slanderous. To be safe, make only factual, emotionless comments. Contact your attorney if you have any doubts. Once left, Feedback **cannot be retracted or edited** by you or by eBay.

Please try to resolve any disputes with the other party before publicly declaring a complaint.

3. Enter your own User ID in the Your Registered User ID box and your password in the Your Password box. The User ID of the individual for whom you want to leave feedback is pre-entered in the User ID of person who you are commenting on box. Enter a transaction number in the Item Number box if your comments relate to a transaction you had with this person.

4. Select the Positive, Negative, or Neutral radio button to rate your experience with the person. Then enter your comments of 80 characters or less in the Your Comment text box. Click the Leave Comment button. The eBay Leaving Feedback for *[User ID]* page appears, confirming that eBay has received your comments.

You don't always need to comment on a specific transaction. You can, for example, describe the quality of the person's auction sales, the reasonableness of his or her prices or bids, or the visual quality of the auction images he or she posts.

Remember

The feedback that you leave is necessarily brief, but make sure that your comments are specific, nonabusive, and descriptive.

If you have second thoughts about any feedback that you leave, you can amend your comments. You can also make a rebuttal or add additional information to feedback about yourself that others leave. You can find out how to do so at `pages.ebay.com/aw/feedback-mock-up.html`.

The eBay Café

Many eBay users have similar interests, such as collecting antiques or other objects. A set of message boards within the eBay site, one of which is called the *eBay Café* (see Figure 7-3), provides a way to discuss such shared interests.

Figure 7-3:   Users regularly meet and greet one another by posting questions and comments on eBay Café message boards.

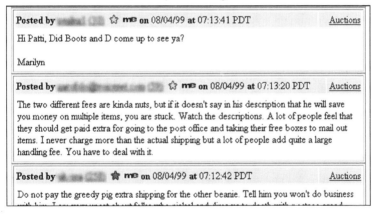

The Café and other boards for specialized topics enable eBay users to get to know each other well by using them frequently. To use the message boards, follow these steps:

1. Click the <u>News/Chat</u> link that appears at the top of nearly every eBay page.

2. Scroll down the page, and click the link for the eBay Café or another forum. You can also go directly to the News and Chat page at `pages.ebay.com/aw/newschat.html`.

3. To post a message yourself, fill out the form at the top of the message board page and then click the Save My Message button.

Remember

The eBay Café provides discussions, but it isn't a chat room. The Café consists of a series of messages boards, some of general interest and others for specific topics. (On a *message board*, the communication doesn't occur in real time as it does in a chat room: You have a bit more lag time between posting a message and viewing it. The eBay Café, therefore, is more like a bulletin board where you post notes and messages than like a real-time discussion.)

eBay Life

eBay's own monthly newsletter, *eBay Life,* is a good source of information. Although *eBay Life* doesn't provide the true "insider" view of eBay that you get on the Cafe and other message boards, it offers profiles of individual users and success stories that can give you ideas for your own transactions.

To find *eBay Life,* point your Web browser to `pages.ebay.com/aw/ebay-life-pA1.html`. The opening page of the newsletter appears, as shown in Figure 7-4.

Figure 7-4: *eBay Life* is essential reading for anyone wanting to master eBay and learn its ins and outs.

August 1999 **ebaY Life**

Writing Your Listing Descriptions For Fun ... and More Profit!

Bidders: Have you seen a listing description that made you grin, smile or laugh outright until your sides ached? Were you tempted to bid on an item just for the entertainment value of the listing?

Sellers: Have you promoted your own auction by creating prose that would make William Shakespeare proud of thee?

A cleverly written description can mean the difference between getting no bids and getting enough bids to generate a **HOT!** icon. (A hot icon appears next to an item following the placement of a 31st bid, and the listing is placed in a special "hot" listings category.)

Barbara tells us why prenuptial shopping and eBay are a match made in heaven!

Disabled single mom says goodbye to Social Services and hello to eBay!

Pay particular attention to the following sections of *eBay Life*:

■ "Greatest eBay Find" presents stories of treasures purchased at eBay sales.

■ "Has eBay Changed Your Life?" relates success stories.

■ "About Me Showcase" contains links to notable Web pages that eBay members created.

Don't be shy about submitting comments to *eBay Life* yourself. Click the link here in the section entitled `We need your help!!!` near the bottom of the newsletter's front page to find out more.

Giving to Charitable Causes

An important part of being a member of a community is helping out and giving back. eBay enables users to do some good by bidding on charity items. Knowing about these items is useful if only to get the complete picture of what the site offers.

eBay regularly conducts charity auctions, for example, to benefit TV talk-show host Rosie O'Donnell's For All Kids Foundation. To find out about these auctions, you can click the <u>For All Kids Foundation!</u> hyperlink on the eBay home page. Or just go directly to `members.ebay.com/aboutme/ 4allkids`.

Longtime fans of singer Jimmy Buffet operate the Virtual Parrot Head Club (VPHC.com), which also conducts charity auctions on eBay. To find the club, just access the eBay Classifieds Search page (at `pages.ebay.com/aw/ search.html`), enter **charity** or **for Parrot Head Club** in the Title Search text box, and then click the Search button. If you entered **charity**, you get back a list of charity auctions and sites that discuss charity-related subjects. If you entered for **Parrot Head Club**, you get back a list of auctions held by the Parrot Head Club.

CHAPTER 8
BECOMING A VIRTUAL AUCTIONEER

IN THIS CHAPTER

- Applying to conduct sales on eBay
- Holding your auction sales
- Specifying the terms for your auction

You can become a seller on eBay whether you're a student, a senior citizen, a sales clerk, a CEO, or anything else — you simply must be 18 years old. You don't need any prior experience to act as your own auctioneer. If you want to be successful and gain a good reputation in the eBay community, however, you must learn quickly how to perform the services that merchants have provided for centuries: marketing merchandise, providing customer service, and fulfilling transactions quickly and efficiently.

This chapter leads you through the process of selling on eBay. Whether your goal is to unload items for a few extra dollars or to sell to collectors or enthusiasts willing pay top dollar, you learn how to set your terms and track bids like an experienced eBay seller.

Reviewing Your eBay Account

Your first step in becoming an eBay seller is to become a registered eBay user — a process that I detail in Chapter 2. eBay then simply charges the fees for listing your items and commissions from the sale of your items to your regular eBay account. You don't need to fill out a special seller's registration form.

You can view the status of your account at any time by following these steps:

1. Connect to the Internet, launch your Web browser, and access the eBay Account Status Web page (click Services ☞ buying and selling on the navigation bar and then click the <u>Check my seller account status</u> link). The eBay Account Status page appears, with a form that you need to fill out so you can review your account (see Figure 8-1).

Figure 8-1:   You can view the status of your account by filling out this form.

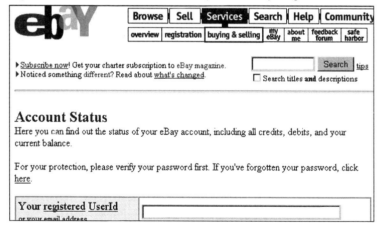

2. Enter your User ID and password in the form shown in Figure 8-1. Fill out the remainder of the form to limit the account information that you see to a particular time period.

3. Click the View Account button at the bottom of the form. The Account Status for *[Your User ID]* page appears. If you haven't yet sold anything on eBay, you see the heading Your account has not yet been created.

You also see a message informing you that, although you do have an eBay account, your account isn't active until you actually incur a fee on eBay. If you have sold something, you will see a list of your sales and a report on any credits you have received and debits that you owe eBay.

Auction Selling: Step-by-Step

After you register as an eBay user, you can begin creating auction listings. You do so by filling out a form in which you describe your auction item, set prices, and include the Web address of any images that you want to accompany your description.

Before you access the form and start filling out your description, however, you need to decide what you want to sell and how much you want for it, as I describe in the following two sections. (You may also want to write down a brief description before starting to fill out the form; see the section "Creating auction descriptions," later in this chapter, for more information.)

Step 1: Decide what to sell

You can easily answer the question "Is my item going to sell on eBay?" by doing some shopping for similar items. Enter the brand name, model number, or other identifying data about your object (or any object, for that matter) in the Search text box on the eBay home page, as shown in Figure 8-2. Compare your item to what others are already offering. Decide, too, on a category where you're likely to find shoppers with an interest in your merchandise.

Figure 8-2:   The eBay Search box.

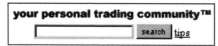

The cost of putting something up for sale on eBay is nominal, unless you're selling something massive, such as a house. You don't have much to lose by offering your item for sale, even if you can't find anything like it currently offered on the eBay site.

Step 2: Set the price

You don't need to be a professional appraiser to determine a reasonable price. For most eBay auctions, you don't actually tell potential bidders how much you want to get for your item. Sellers need to take one of the following two actions:

- You can put the object up for auction without setting a reserve price and let the market (that is, the bidders) determine the final value. Announce in your listing that you're specifying "No Reserve," (it's common to announce the lack of a reserve using these words) and you're likely to get lots of bids from shoppers looking for a potential bargain.

- You can specify a reserve price. If you want, you can keep the reserve price secret from bidders until someone places a bid that meets or attains it. (I explain reserve prices in more detail in Chapter 4.)

If you sell without a reserve, you must sell the item to the highest bidder (although you can end your sale early without selling to anyone, as I describe in Chapter 9). If you specify a reserve, you must sell the item only if someone offers your desired price.

You may get the idea that reserve price auctions are always better for sellers. Many sellers, however, report that items without a reserve attract more bids and often result in sale prices that exceed the amount the seller would have specified as a reserve.

Although you can make it so, your reserve price doesn't *need* to remain a secret. Some eBay sellers reveal their reserve right in their auction description. Others set a minimum bid that represents what they ultimately want. If the seller wants to get at least $250 for an object, for example, he enters that amount as the minimum bid in the Minimum Bid text box on the List New Item form. Bidding then starts, in effect, with the seller's desired price.

Setting your minimum bid as the least amount you're willing to take often discourages users, because they don't believe that they can get a bargain. Often the sale ends with no one ever placing any bids.

If you aren't sure what an item is worth, go to the local library and look its value up in a price guide. Or check out the Web for an online appraisal from the International Society of Appraisers (at `www.isa-appraisers.org/search.htm`). The appraiser you hire will charge you either an hourly fee, a flat rate, or a separate charge for each item appraised.

Some of the Web sites that traditional auction houses operate provide appraisal services directly to individuals selling items online. Butterfield & Butterfield, which eBay owns, for example, provides e-mail appraisals based on an image of the sale item that you send to the auction house. Go to the company's Web site (at `www.butterfields.com`) and click the <u>Appraisal Services</u> link at the bottom of the page.

Step 3: Find the right category for selling

If you're preparing to put something up for auction on eBay, you tend to look at categories from a different perspective than that of a buyer. Your job now is to find the category in which you're most likely to find interested bidders for your item — individuals who're already looking for what you're offering or who, after they spot your listing, are sure to realize that they simply must have it, even if they've never considered this fact before.

The Sell Your Item form that you use to list sales items (click on the **Sell** link on the navigation bar to access this form) includes a Choose a Category area, but it doesn't give you much help in choosing the category that's right for you. It simply presents you with a series of drop-down lists from which you can choose the best category available (see Figure 8-3).

Figure 8-3: If you list an auction item for sale, you must select the category in which you want the listing to appear.

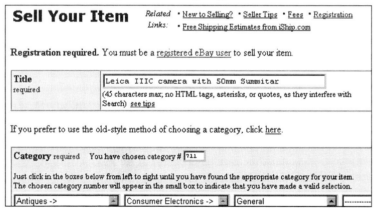

The simplest way to find an appropriate category is to search for items that are similar or identical to yours that are already up for sale on eBay. At the top of each auction-listing page, you find a hypertext link displaying the name of the current category, such as <u>Coins:US:Commemorative</u>. If you spot several items similar to yours in the same category, you can be pretty certain that it's the right one for your item.

Step 4: Fill out the rest of the Sell Your Item form

Many of the categories in the Sell Your Item form include instructions that tell you how best to fill them out. Following are some more brief suggestions for filling out some of these categories:

- **Title:** A good title is essential because that's what turns up in lists of auction items that buyers obtain from a search. (See Chapter 3 for more information on search eBay.) Keep your title to no more than five or six words and mention any model numbers that collectors use to identify what they're looking for. Avoid using tired terms such as **!!!L@@K!!!**, which appear so often that they have virtually no effect on buyers anymore.

- **Category:** The eBay site includes hundreds of different categories. In which one should your item appear? Search for objects that are similar to yours and see in what categories they turn up. Place your items in a category with similar objects.

- **Picture URL:** *URL* stands for Uniform Resource Locator, a standard form of address that you use to locate any object or Web site available on the Internet. You get the URL for your image from the site that hosts it (eBay does not host image files for you). Suppose, for example, that your directory on America Online hosts the photo of what you're selling. That directory uses the URL `members.aol.com/username`, and the file name of the image is `object.jpg`. The URL that you enter in the Picture URL text box for the image of your item, therefore, is `members.aol.com/username/object.jpg`. See Chapter 10 for more details about adding images.

■ **Minimum Bid:** A minimum bid is where you want the bidding to start. Pick a small starting point, such as $1, for the minimum bid. If you have something you absolutely refuse to sell for less than a certain amount, you can specify that amount as the minimum bid. Be aware, however, that you're very likely to discourage bidders by setting a sizable minimum and don't be surprised if the auction ends without a single bid coming in.

■ **Duration:** Seven days is the most common auction period, but you can select an auction term of three, five, or ten days as well.

The most important part of your auction listing (along with the title) is its description, which I describe in the following section.

Step 5: Write a good description of your item

In a traditional (non-Internet) auction, an auction catalog describes any objects for sale, and the auctioneer mentions an object's outstanding features just before taking bids. On eBay, you must market and describe your won merchandise by filling out the Description text box of the Sell Your Item form. An effective description embodies the following characteristics:

■ **Brief but complete:** The more details that you provide, the better are your chances of getting bids. The Description section of the Sell Your Item form doesn't specify a limit to the number of words that you can enter.

■ **Positive:** Say what's special about the item. If what you're selling is especially rare or has a desirable feature — it's a solid gold watch rather than a gold-plated one, for example — say so in your description.

■ **Honest:** Make sure that your listing is complete and accurate. Don't be reluctant to mention any defects in what you're selling. Doing so shows people that you're honest, and prevents disputes after you ship the item. The more details that you provide, the better are your chances of getting bids. Be specific, too. Remember that avid collectors who are knowledgeable about brand names and model numbers are looking for specific items to fill out their collections.

You need a good description to maximize the number of bids you receive. A good description helps potential buyers decide whether your merchandise is of interest to them.

As the instructions just below the Description text box point out, you can add HyperText Markup Language (HTML) instructions to your description to highlight certain words or phrases by making them bold, for example, or italic.

Step 6: Review and submit the Sell Your Item form

After you complete the Sell Your Item form, you click the Review button at the bottom of the form. The eBay New Item Verification page appears, presenting the information you just entered so that you can verify that everything's how you want it to look (see Figure 8-4).

Figure 8-4: Make sure that you check your description for any typos or other mistakes before it goes online.

```
Current account balance before adding this item: $0.00.

Please verify your entry as it appears below. If there are any errors, please use the back button on
your browser to go back and correct your entry. Once you are satisfied with the entry, please
press the submit button.

Your User ID:                    gholden@interaccess.com
The title of the item:           Leica IIIC camera with 50mm Summitar
Optional boldface title:         no
Featured auction:                no
Featured category auction:       no
Great Gift auction:              no
Optional Gallery:                no
Optional Featured Gallery:       no
The category of the item:        Photo & Electronics:Photo Equipment:Vintage,
Optional reserve price:          $500.00
Optional private auction:        no
Bidding starts at:               $1.00
```

Although you can edit your description and add information after the sale begins, you're best off avoiding mistakes the first time that you submit this information. (See the section "Editing auction descriptions," later in this chapter, for information on how to fix errors later.)

If your description is correct, click the Submit My Listing button at the bottom of the New Item Verification page to start your auction. A good idea at this point is to wait a few minutes and then conduct a search for your auction title to view your listing right away. You can thereby make sure that the description appears correctly, including any images you specified for the listing.

If your description is incorrect or you decide not to put your sale online after all, click the Click here to cancel hyperlink at the bottom of the New Item Verification page. You must then reenter your description from scratch if you decide to list it again later.

If you have an image of your item that you intend to post along with your description, make sure that the image is already posted on your image hosting site (see Chapter 10) and that you entered the image URL correctly in the Sell Your Item form. If the URL is wrong or if you haven't yet posted your image, a generic question mark icon appears instead of your actual image. If the URL is wrong, make sure it matches the URL of your image exactly. If the image isn't posted yet, put it online, then reconnect to your auction listing page to make sure it appears correctly.

CHAPTER 9

AFTER YOUR AUCTION STARTS

IN THIS CHAPTER

- Changing auction listings after your sale starts
- Contacting high bidders and receiving payment
- Being aware of auction fees for sellers

Putting an item up for auction on eBay is easy. Sometimes, completing the sale requires more work than simply starting it. But the reward for your work is the payment you receive from the high bidder and positive feedback you receive. This chapter examines how to reap those rewards.

Editing Auction Descriptions

After your description goes online, you can expect to field questions from interested customers. If you get several similar questions about an item, consider adding the answer to your description. Although your sale is still going on, you have the right at any time to change the item's category or add information to your original description.

In fact, as long as no one's yet placed a bid, you can even rewrite a description or title entirely, edit the payment or shipping terms, or add or change an image. You can edit your listing by accessing `pages.ebay.com/services/buyandsell/add-to-item.html` and filling out the Adding to Your Item Description form shown in Figure 9-1.

Figure 9-1: After your sale goes online, you can change or add to your description or even add a photo.

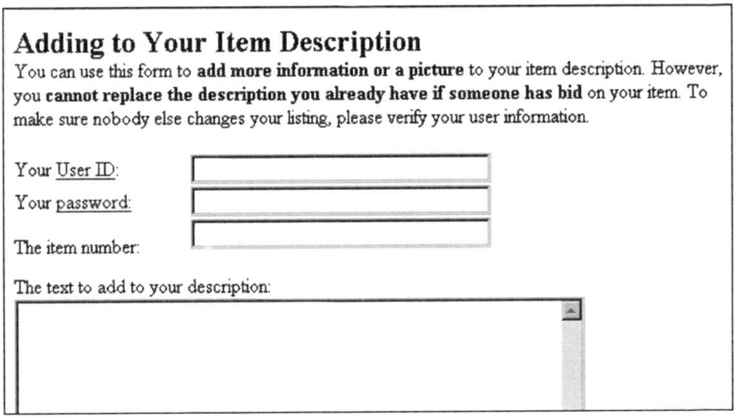

Adding to Your Item Description

You can use this form to **add more information or a picture** to your item description. However, you **cannot replace the description you already have if someone has bid** on your item. To make sure nobody else changes your listing, please verify your user information.

Your User ID: [   ]

Your password: [   ]

The item number: [   ]

The text to add to your description:

[   ]

Processing Sales

Processing the sale means giving the item to the buyer and receiving payment for that item. After the auction ends, contact your winner(s) promptly — preferably within the hour but at least within one day. Along with offering your congratulations to the winners, give them directions for paying you.

After you receive payment, make sure that you send a quick e-mail acknowledgment that you've received the credit card payment or check.

Tell the winning bidder exactly when you're sending out the shipment. A good business practice is to ship your item the same day that the payment clears your bank. (Most banks will let you know if a check has cleared either by phone or in person.) Try not to wait any longer than a week after the payment clears, or you risk getting negative feedback from the high bidder.

Reselling Items

Most items that you put up for auction on eBay do sell. (eBay estimates the exact number at 70 percent.) Many others, however, don't sell. You don't, however, need to give up trying to sell the item just because it doesn't sell the first time that you offer it. You may attract more (or higher) bids later by taking such steps as providing better images, changing the title or description, or removing the reserve price.

eBay does charge you a second insertion fee for relisting, but if your item sells the second time around, eBay refunds the second insertion fee. (If it doesn't sell the second time, you are required to pay the insertion fee). You can relist your item if the following conditions apply:

- You didn't receive any bids at all and you held a regular auction (not a reserve price auction).

- Fewer than thirty days have passed since the closing date of the first auction. (If you wait any longer, eBay will not refund your insertion fee if the item sells.)

- You didn't receive any bids that met or exceeded your reserve price if you originally specified one.

To relist your item, return to the completed auction-item page and click the <u>Now that the auction has ended, you can easily relist this item by clicking here</u> hyperlink. If your item sells the second time around, eBay refunds the second insertion fee you had to pay. (This refund policy, however, doesn't apply to Dutch auctions; see Chapter 4 for more information about how Dutch auctions work.)

Ending Your Auction Early

Suppose that you have second thoughts about offering an item for sale. Sometimes, you may get a better offer from a friend or relative who's not on eBay, or you may decide that you simply can't part with the item after all.

If you decide not to sell the item after all, you can end the sale before the "formal" end of the auction. But to do so, you must pay two prices. One is monetary: You still must pay eBay the insertion fee for the item as well as a final value fee based on the highest bid for your item. The second price that you pay is the potential damage you may incur to your reputation: Any eBay users who already placed bids before you cancel the auction may well submit negative feedback about you.

End your auction early by clicking **Services ☞ buying & selling** on the navigation bar and then clicking the End my auction early hyperlink. A form appears that allows you to end your auction (see Figure 9-2). Fill in your eBay ID, your password, and the item number of the auction and click the End Auction button.

Figure 9-2: The End Your Auction Early form.

eBay Ending Auction - Netscape

File Edit View Go Communicator Help

Ending Your Auction

You can use this form if you want to end your auction early. But remember, lots of bidders wait until the very last minute to bid—they're trying to avoid being outbid!—so you may lose a potential buyer by ending your auction early.

If you are ending the auction because you no longer wish to sell your item, you must cancel all bids on your auction before it ends. If you do not do so, you are obligated to sell to the high bidder.

Your User ID:

Your password:

The item number:

Document: Done

If you do cancel a sale, personally contact each of the bidders for the item to extend your apologies and explain your reasons for ending the sale early. This approach may prevent some negative feedback.

Paying eBay

If all you've done so far is to buy items on eBay, you may wonder how eBay makes money on its auctions. Well, eBay makes its money from the people who sell items on the site. The seller must pay a fee before the sale to list the item for auction and then pays a percentage of the proceeds after the sale is complete.

Insertion fees

eBay charges members a nominal fee, known as an *insertion fee*, to list objects for sale. eBay bases this fee either on the reserve price that you specify for an item or, if you don't use a reserve, the opening-value or minimum-bid price that you specify at the time that you first list the item. (These prices are part of the Sell Your Item form that you fill out to place an item for sale on eBay, as I describe in Chapter 8.)

Typical insertion fees (based on rates that eBay is charging as I write this book) appear in Table 9-1. eBay charges fixed rates for cars and trucks that you put up for auction. You incur additional insertion fees if you want to place your listing in a special featured location on the site.

Make sure that you read about the company's insertion fees and commissions on eBay's User Agreement – Fees and Credits page (at `pages.ebay.com/aw/agreement-fees.html`).

Table 9-1: eBay Insertion Fees

Opening Value/ Reserve Price	Insertion Fee
$0.01–$9.99	$0.25
$10–$24.99	$0.50
$25–$49.99	$1
$50 and up	$2

Remember

You must pay the insertion fee whether you successfully complete the transaction or not.

You may fail to complete a sale if any of the following situations occur:

■ No one bids on your item.

■ You decide to cancel the sale because you have second thoughts or found another buyer. (I describe the cancellation process in the section "Ending your auction immediately," later in this chapter.)

■ You specify a reserve price (one that, if no one meets or exceeds it, removes your obligation to sell the item; see Chapter 6) and the reserve is not met.

Final value fees (commissions)

The *final value fee* is a commission that eBay charges sellers after they make a sale. eBay charges a percentage of the selling price on an item for use of its auction service. eBay calculates the percentage on a "stepped" basis. That is, the final value fee is not a flat fee, but has to be calculated in several steps, which are detailed in Table 9-2 on the following page:

Table 9-2:   Final Value Fees

If the Final Bid Is...	Calculate the Final Value Fee Like This	For This Final Bid	You Would Figure
$25 or less	Multiply the final bid by .05. Round this number to the nearest penny.	$22.50	$22.50 × .05 = $1.125 Final Value Fee = $1.13
$25.01@nd$1000	Subtract $25 from the final bid. Multiply the result by .025. Add $1.25 to that number and round to the nearest penny.	$780	$780 − $25 = $755 $755 × .025 = $18.875 $18.875 + $1.25 = $20.125 Final Value Fee = $20.13
$1000.01 or more	Subtract $1000 from the final bid. Multiply the result by .0125. Add $25.63 to that number and round to the nearest penny.	$2,800	$2,800 − $1,000 = $1,800 $1,800 × .0125 = $22.50 $22.50 + $25.63 = $48.13 Final Value Fee = $48.13

On Dutch auctions, you multiply the lowest qualifying bid by the number of items sold. If you sell ten items, for example, and the lowest qualifying bid is $150, the final value is $1,500. You'd calculate the final value fee for this auction by subtracting $1000 from the final value to get $500. Multiplying $500 by .0125 gives you $6.25. Adding $25.63 to $6.25 gives you a final value fee of $31.88.

Remember

You don't pay a final value fee if nobody bids on your auction, if no one meets your reserve price, or if you list your item in eBay's Real Estate category. However, if you end your sale early and there were bids on the item, you are charged a final value fee.

Paying the fees

After you sell something on eBay, you need to pay the service's insertion fees and final value fees. eBay members can accumulate up to $10 worth of fees in their account before they must pay off their bill. If you owe eBay money, you receive an invoice by e-mail. eBay sends out its invoices on the first day of each month. You can review the fees that you currently owe eBay by reviewing your online account information.

Next, decide how you want to pay. You can set up your account so that eBay automatically charges any fees to your credit card. You can also pay each time by check, or money order. Paying invoices as they arrive particularly makes sense if you sell only occasionally.

To settle your eBay account by having eBay automatically deduct charges from your credit card, you must put your credit card on file with eBay at `arribada.ebay.com/aw-secure/cc-update.html`.

If you'd rather pay each time you receive an invoice, obtain a payment voucher at `pages.ebay.com/aw/pay-coupon.html` and mail the payment to eBay. You can read more about payment options by reviewing the "Payment Terms" section of the User Agreement – Fees and Credits page (at `pages.ebay.com/aw/agreement-fees.html`).

CHAPTER 10

ADDING IMAGES TO EBAY LISTINGS

IN THIS CHAPTER

- Understanding digital images and Web page image formats
- Capturing images to illustrate your sales items
- Finding a Web host for your auction images

You can present items for auction on eBay without images that effectively give bidders the chance to "inspect the merchandise" before making an offer. If you do so, however, you're expecting people to bid sight unseen. A nice image, on the other hand, makes items you're offering for sale seem far more attractive to prospective bidders. Shoppers are much more likely to make inquiries and place bids if they can inspect one or more good images before hand.

Unless the object you're offering is especially desirable, an image is almost a requirement if you want to maximize bids and gain top dollar for what you hope to sell. In this chapter, I explain the process of adding images to your sales descriptions on eBay.

Capturing Digital Images

Capturing a digital image refers to converting an image to a format that a computer can display, edit, or otherwise process. In capturing an image, a *scanner* or *digital camera* turns the image into very small squares, known as *pixels*. Each pixel in a computer image contains one or more bits of digital information.

If you open a computer image file in a graphics program and zoom in on it, you can see the pixels. Figure 10-1 shows an original computer graphic image and a close-up view of its individual pixels.

Figure 10-1:   Digital images consist of pixels.

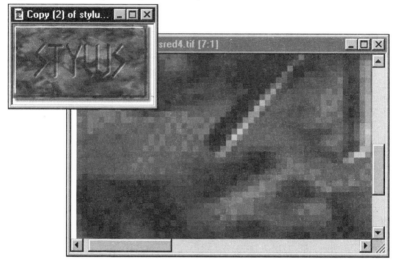

Options for capturing images

You have four options for obtaining digital images of your auction objects. The one that you choose depends on the time available, your budget, and the tools you already have available. The following list describes the methods available to you:

■ **Scan the image:** Scanners are a cost-effective option these days, as some scanners are available for $100 or less. You can also rent time on a scanner at a branch of Kinko's Copies. Or you can borrow a friend's scanning device. Simply take a conventional photo of an object with a camera and scan the image to convert it to the computer file. This is the most time-consuming option.

If you happen to be selling an object that's flat, such as a book, you can scan it in directly without first taking a photograph.

■ **Use a photo lab:** You can take a conventional print or slide photo and have the photo lab return the images to you on computer disk instead of as prints or slides.

■ **Take a digital photo:** If you have access to one, you can use a digital camera to take a photo of what you want to sell. The camera saves the image directly to computer disk. Digital cameras are still fairly pricey (in the $400–$800 range), but this is the fastest option.

■ **Capture a video image of the object and convert the image to digital format:** Some digital video cameras are available that can save images directly to disk (for a whopping amount of money). You can also use a conventional camcorder and then convert the image by using Snappy Video Snapshot by Play Incorporated (find out about these devices at www.play.com/products/snappy/index.html).

Choosing a graphics format

For presentation on the Web, you need to put your graphics in digital format and you need to compress them in size as well. Such files appear in a Web browser window in their decompressed state. In contrast to other aspects of graphics creation, the question of what format to use for your own images is relatively simple; only two compression methods are in wide use for Web graphics today: *GIF* and *JPEG*. All Web browsers can open and display files in these formats. Of these two, eBay recommends that you save your image in JPEG format.

JPEG stands for *Joint Photographic Experts Group* and compresses an image differently than does than GIF. But without getting too technical about it, JPEG generally works better for black-and-white or color photos than GIF does.

Both GIF and JPEG images display correctly on eBay auction pages. JPEG, however, is generally a better format for photographic images with lots of colors, while GIF generally works better for line drawings.

If you hire someone to either scan or capture the image for you, you can tell the person to save the files as JPEGs. Otherwise, you can do so yourself by using the software that comes with your scanner, digital camera, or other hardware device. Usually, you save in JPEG format by choosing File⟿Save from the program's menu bar and then choosing JPEG from the list of formats that are available. You also need to save the file with the file name extension JPG (or, on a Macintosh, JPEG).

JPEG compresses image files, but it provides you with several different levels of compression from which to choose. The higher the level of compression, the smaller the image file. This is good, because smaller images appear on your prospective buyers' computer screens more quickly than big, bloated ones.

If you use Maximum compression, you lose some information in the image, and the image doesn't appear as sharp as it can if you use a lower level of compression. Although using Low compression results in images with a bigger file size, the sharpness and color of the images come out better. If you're not sure which level to choose, try High or Maximum compression to keep the file size as small as possible.

Finding a host for your images

eBay posts your descriptions and auction terms online. eBay doesn't however, provide you with space for your accompanying auction images. To include your image, you must find another site or *host* with a Web server that can host your digital image file (that is, one that enables you to place the file in a directory on the server so that someone with a Web browser can access them).

The following list describes some of the types of Web hosts that you can use to make your auction image files available online:

- **Your own ISP:** The first place to turn is to the company that gives you access to the Internet: your internet service provider (ISP). Providing users with access to the Internet and hosting Web sites are two different functions, certainly, but the same organization may well perform them. Many ISPs provide you with use of at least 10MB of Web site space at no additional cost to you.

- **America Online (AOL):** AOL is a commercial online provider: It provides subscribers with access to its own online content as well as a way to connect to the wider Internet. It also enables subscribers to create and publish their own Web pages or to place simple image files on the Web. AOL is quite popular with sellers on eBay and other auction services.

- **A free Web hosting service:** Some Web sites are in the business of providing individuals with free e-mail accounts, easy-to-use software for creating Web pages, and space for posting images and Web pages online. One of the most popular such services is Yahoo! GeoCities (at `www.geocities.com`), which allocates each of its users a generous 11MB of Web space as well as a point-and-click tool known as GeoBuilder that helps you create your home page quickly on its server. Other such resources include Tripod (at `www.tripod.com`) and XOOM.com (at `xoom.com/home`).

- **A photo hosting service:** A few Web sites specialize in providing space where eBay and other auction users can publish auction images to accompany sales listings. These sites aren't free, however. PixHost (at `www.pixhost.com`), for example, enables you to host two images on its site for free; after that trial usage, hosting images cost 50 cents each for 30 days. You may also want to visit Imagehost (at `www.imagehost.com`), a site that eBay sellers often use.

Before paying a service to host your Web site, check to determine whether your ISP provides the service as part of your monthly access fee. If your ISP charges extra to host Web content and you aren't concerned with creating Web sites, go with one of the free services to host your images instead of paying a Web hosting fee.

Adding Images to Your eBay Listing

After you create a digital image and add it to your host site, you add that image to your sales description by specifying the URL for the image on the eBay Sell Your Item form (see Chapter 8). All ISPs provide customers with instructions on how to figure out their Web page URLs. Call the Customer Service section of your ISP, or check the company's FAQ.

A common convention is to assign a URL that looks like this (this example is for a JPEG image, which has the filename extension .jpg; a GIF image should end with .gif):

```
http://www.yourISP.com/~yourusername/
filename.jpg
```

You can also specify whether to place any images that accompany your listing in the eBay Gallery as well as displaying them on the auction Web page itself.

The Gallery is a collection of images that auction sellers submit of items they're currently offering for sale (see Figure 10-2). Buyers can browse through the images and click one in which they're interested; clicking the image takes them to the auction sales page where they can read a description and place a bid if they so choose. The Gallery doesn't display all the images that accompany auction listings — only the ones for which sellers pay the extra 25-cent fee for extra exposure in the Gallery. (You can splurge and pay $19.95 to place your image in a featured area of the Gallery as well.)

Figure 10-2: For a small extra fee, your images can get some exposure in the eBay Gallery.

The images that appear in the Gallery are *thumbnails* — miniature versions of the full-sized images. Shoppers who have slow Internet connections (such as a 14.4 Kbps or 28.8 Kbps modems) may find that Gallery images take too long to appear on-screen and opt for browsing auction listings either by searching or clicking through hierarchies, as I describe in Chapter 3.

Only images that you save in JPEG format can appear in the Gallery; you must convert GIF images to JPEGs by using a graphics program such as Paint Shop Pro for Windows (at www.jasc.com) or GraphicConverter for the Macintosh, which is available from Tucows (at www.tucows.com) and other shareware sites.

Tips for Creating Images That Sell

An important part of selling at auction is providing a good image that attracts attention and helps people decide whether what you're offering is a good match for what they need.

Often, images aren't good if you capture them straight from your scanner, digital camera, or other input device. Instead, after you save your image in JPEG or GIF format, you can then edit (or, in photographic terms, *retouch*) the image in a graphics program to improve its appearance. Following are two of the simplest ways to create good images:

■ **Adjust contrast and brightness:** The *contrast* of an image is the degree of difference between its light and dark tones. *Brightness* refers to the vibrancy or energy of the colors or shades of color in the image. Images displaying adequate levels of contrast are easier to view on a monitor.

■ **Keep file size small:** One of the most courteous things that you can do for your auction customers is to give their Web browsers small, "byte-sized" files that don't make their browsers labor too long to display the images. One of the best ways to keep an image within a small file size is to keep it as small as possible in its physical dimensions as well. Resize the image so that it's smaller than originally scanned and fits well on the eBay auction Web page. (Look through your graphics program's menus to find a resize option.)

Generally speaking, an image that's two or three inches wide and perhaps four to five inches tall is a good size. File sizes of 20 to 30K or less are also desirable.

■ **Zoom in on what's important:** *Cropping* refers to the practice of cutting out unnecessary details and keeping a certain area of the image on which you want to focus. It makes the image size smaller so that the photo fits better in a Web browser window. By making the image smaller, you also make the file size smaller. An image that's, say, 12K in size appears on-screen much faster than one that's 100K in size.

After posting an image online, verify that it actually appears on your page. The most common cause of a broken image or question mark icon appearing with your description instead of the image itself is an incorrect URL. If you're typing the URL from scratch, you must get it exactly right: A single blank space, capital letter, or typo in an URL can prevent a Web browser from locating the image and displaying it on-screen.

eBay posts a bulletin-board page where you can ask questions about adding images to auction listings and get help from other eBay users. Go to the eBay Site Map page (click on the link site map at the top of any eBay page), scroll down to the eBay Bulletin Boards area of the page, and click the Help with Images and HTML hyperlink.

CLIFFSNOTES REVIEW

Use this CliffsNotes Review to practice what you've learned in this book and to build your confidence in doing the job right the first time. After you work through the review questions, the problem-solving exercises, the visual test, and the fun and useful practice projects, you're well on your way to achieving your goal of buying and selling successfully on eBay.

Q&A

1. What highlighted link on the home page takes you to the area of the eBay site where you can change your password?

   a. Register it's fun and free
   b. Help
   c. Services

2. What do you click on to view feedback for a seller whose username is followed by (6), a blue star, and the heading "me"?

   a. me
   b. (6)
   c. the star

3. Name two ways to locate an item on eBay.

   _____

   _____

4. Which of the following statements about proxy bidding is false?

   a. It is only available on reserve price auctions.
   b. It lets the bidder place bids without being at a computer.
   c. The bidder may not end up paying the maximum amount of the proxy bid.

5. Explain how someone wins a Dutch auction.

   _____

   _____

   _____

Answers: (1) b. (2) b. (3) The Search feature, and clicking through categories. (4) a. (5) The "winner" is anyone who bids the same or higher than the lowest qualifying bid, because they pay only the amount of the lowest qualifying bid.

Scenarios

1. The current high bid for an item is $100. You bid $125. However, immediately after you place your bid, someone else (not you) is listed as the high bidder at $127.50. What is the most likely cause? _____

2. You send off a check for an item you have purchased. You are unable to reach the seller by e-mail. You should _____
_____.

3. You see an auction item you know a friend will want to bid on. To let your friend know about it, you e-mail the auction listing by _____.

Answers: (1) The previous high bidder placed a proxy bid higher than $125, and the bid increment is $2.50. (2) Contact eBay's SafeHarbor and file a complaint with a consumer fraud organization. (3) Clicking on the <u>mail this auction to a friend</u> link on the auction listing page.

Visual Test

1. <u>recoll</u> (494) ☆ me
Click the me image to view the _____
_____.

Click the seller's name to _____
_____.

2.

What can you do when you see this image instead of an image of a sale item you want to bid on? _____

_____

_____

Answers: (1) seller's Web page; send him or her an e-mail message. (2) Ask the seller to e-mail you a new image.

Consider This

■ Did you know that service outages and changes to the eBay site are explained on the eBay Announcement Board?

■ Did you know that eBay auctions are archived so you can review what past items have sold for?

■ Did you know that Featured Auctions are not necessarily special, but the seller simply pays an extra fee to feature items?

CLIFFSNOTES RESOURCE CENTER

The learning doesn't need to stop here. CliffsNotes Resource Center shows you the best of the best — links to the best information in print and online about eBay and the Internet. And don't think that this is all we've prepared for you; we've put all kinds of pertinent information at www.cliffsnotes.com. Look for all the terrific resources at your favorite bookstore or local library and on the Internet. When you're online, make your first stop www.cliffsnotes.com where you'll find more incredibly useful information about eBay.

Books

This CliffsNotes book is one of many great books about cool stuff you can do online that's published by IDG Books Worldwide, Inc. So when you're ready to expand your knowledge of the things virtual, check out some of these publications:

Teach Yourself the Internet and the World Wide Web VISUALLY. A good next step for someone who learns better by seeing than by reading would be to get this visually stunning book about using the Internet by Maran Graphics. Find out how to use browsers, FTP, chats, and more by looking at pictures similar to what you see on your computer screen. Don't read about where to click your mouse and why — look at it! (IDG Books Worldwide) $29.99

CliffsNotes Building Your First Web Page. At some point in your eBay career, you may want to build an "About Me" page or apply advanced HTML formatting to your auction descriptions. Alan Simpson, one of the most prolific writers in computerdom, takes you through the Web-page process in a simple, step-by-step manner. (IDG Books Worldwide, Inc.) $8.99

eBay For Dummies. If you want a more in-depth look at the eBay auction system, but one that's still user-friendly and full of tips and useful instructions, check out this new book by in the ...*For Dummies* series (IDG Books Worldwide, Inc.) $19.99

Internet Auctions For Dummies. If you like this CliffsNotes book, you'll love the big book by the same author! Take a look at the whole exploding field of Internet auctions, including eBay. Person-to-person auctions are discussed, as well as company auctions, computer auction services, and personal "home-grown" auctions. (IDG Books Worldwide) $24.99

Digital Photography For Dummies, 2nd Edition. In Chapter 10, I explain the importance of good images in selling your merchandise on eBay. For more information about working with digital images, check out the second edition of *Digital Photography For Dummies* by Julie Adair King. (IDG Books Worldwide) $24.99

Buying Online For Dummies. This book tells you about how to locate the best virtual stores and the right products at the right prices, all from the comfort of your home or office computer. You'll find helpful advice to make secure transactions over the Net, buy and sell through online classified ads, and set up your own Internet connection optimized for online shopping. Be sure to check out this book's 70+ pages of great online outlets and the bonus CD-ROM, which contains shareware and freeware programs to make your online shopping experience fun, safe, and hassle-free. (IDG Books Worldwide) $24.99

Finding books published by IDG Books Worldwide, Inc. is a snap. Check out your favorite bookstore in your town, or go to your favorite online bookseller. You can also check out the following Web sites where the books are available for you to buy:

- www.cliffsnotes.com
- www.dummies.com
- www.idgbooks.com

Internet

Check out these Web sites for more information about eBay and more:

Golden Triangle, golden-triangle.org — If you like participating in eBay auctions that benefit charitable causes, also check out The Golden Triangle site.

Virtual Notions, virtualnotions.com — Purchase software that lets you format eBay auction listings, edit graphics files, and much more.

Blackthorne Software, www.blackthorne.com — Try out and purchase software that helps auction sellers format and track auction listings on eBay.

Geocities, www.geocities.com — Post a Web page on the Internet for free (as long as you abide by the Yahoo! Geocities guidelines).

Center for Online Addiction's Virtual Clinic, www.netaddiction.com/clinic.htm — Are online auctions consuming too much of your time and money? You may be addicted. You can get help at this Web site.

Switchboard.com, www.switchboard.com — Find auction sellers' addresses and phone numbers so you can contact them or verify their identity.

Next time you're on the Internet, don't forget to drop by www.cliffsnotes.com. We created an online Resource Center that you can use today, tomorrow, and beyond.

Magazines & Other Media

The following media offerings can help keep you up to date on eBay and the Internet. Most of these magazines can be found at your neighborhood bookstore. And where these magazines publish online, I provide the Web site URL. Usually magazine Web sites offer some information for free, but to get all the available information, you have to subscribe.

The Industry Standard provides those interested in the business of the Internet complete coverage of the people, jobs, companies, and trends shaping today's Internet economy. (www.thestandard.com) The first four issues are free, and the subscription rate is $49.97 for 40 issues per year.

Wired Magazine provides hip coverage of the online technologies that are transforming our lives. In the words of the publication itself, "It speaks not just to the high-tech professionals and the business savvy, but also to the forward-looking, the culturally astute, and the simply curious. (www.wired.com/wired) The first two issues are free, and the subscription rate is $21.95 for 10 additional issues.

Yahoo! Internet Life is a collaborative publication between Yahoo! and Ziff Davis that keeps you apprised of all the cool — and critically important — developments in the online world. (www.zdnet.com/yil/) The first issue is free, and the subscription rate is $19.99 for 11 additional issues.

Send Us Your Favorite Tips

In your quest for learning, have you ever experienced that sublime moment when you figure out a trick that saves time or trouble? Perhaps you realized you were taking ten steps to accomplish something that could have taken two. Or you found a little-known workaround that gets great results. If you've discovered a useful tip that helped you buy and sell on eBay more effectively and you'd like to share it, the CliffsNotes staff would love to hear from you. Go to our Web site at www.cliffsnotes.com and click the Talk to Us button. If we select your tip, we may publish it as part of CliffsNotes Daily, our exciting, free e-mail newsletter. To find out more or to subscribe to a newsletter, go to on the Web.

INDEX

CliffsNotes™

Your shortcut to success™ for over 40 years

Computers and Software
Confused by computers? Struggling with software? Let *CliffsNotes* get you up to speed on the fundamentals — quickly and easily. Titles include:

Balancing Your Checkbook with Quicken.
Buying Your First PC
Creating a Dynamite PowerPoint® 2000 Presentation
Making Windows. 98 Work for You
Setting up a Windows. 98 Home Network
Upgrading and Repairing Your PC
Using Your First PC
Using Your First iMac.
Writing Your First Computer Program

The Internet
Intrigued by the Internet? Puzzled about life online? Let *CliffsNotes* show you how to get started with e-mail, Web surfing, and more. Titles include:

Buying and Selling on eBay®
Creating Web Pages with HTML
Creating Your First Web Page
Exploring the Internet with Yahoo!®
Finding a Job on the Web
Getting on the Internet
Going Online with AOL®
Shopping Online Safely